RETAIL REFRAME

SAMEER BABBAR

ISBN 978-0-9876408-0-2

Disclaimer

Although the author and publisher have made every effort to ensure that the information in this book was correct at press time, the author and publisher do not assume and hereby disclaim any liability to any party for any loss, damage, or disruption caused by errors or omissions, whether such errors or omissions result from negligence, accident, or any other cause.

This book is dedicated to all those who want to leverage creativity, information and passion to make their mark in business.

Table of Contents

Preface

The first question anyone may ask is why someone goes to do business and if one does, chooses to venture into retail. Each person may have their own motivation. One may want to run it as a hobby while someone else may be looking at solving a problem at a global scale.

Retail is where any business comes face to face with end customer, whether it deals with a commodity or a specialised product.

While in the retail one has to face competing interests, pay for staff, pay for the outlet, purchase items that need to be instrumental in fulfilling customer requirements, pay oneself, invest money back in the business and save for the rainy day as market constantly fluctuates. Being in retail requires being in the epicentre of entire business ecosystem. Hence the term "retail is detail".

Hailing from a family where business was done through generations and overlaid with my experience in decision support and strategic analytics, gave me a new lens to look at businesses.

Perhaps that is one of the key reasons some businesses succeed, and some don't, it hovers around quality of decision in a dynamic environment. Not all decisions will be right however to quickly make new decisions should the circumstances require is the key. One may not always have the right experience to make those decisions which will leave only two options either to learn from your own mistakes or from someone else's.

The motivation you may have is that you want to explore a hobby, help solve your problem and while doing it help others, make life simple on the planet, take humanity to a different problem, make money ...and the list is very long. You will have to write down why you want to get into business, it will give you the underpinning motivation, you have just peeled the first layer of onion, you will then need to find the process behind your motivation the meaning that you are searching for. Often you will find that your true motivation is different. For many who talk about money, their true motivation may be around what money has to offer say freedom or just wanting to satisfy the ego of having more.

It's good to have some knowledge of the industry, we go into. Though I agree that sometimes it is good to have no knowledge, so you do not carry the mindset of what's not possible. More often than less the technical ability is more important to position yourself in your business. This book can only serve as a guide. You may like to surround yourself with mentors and advisors that can watch your back while you embark on your journey.

I have taken focus of brick and mortar stores, to look into retail as the physical stores are the most expensive element in a business. Though with advent of time we have seen more and more businesses go online and resulting significant investment in the online business. Online business and business models deal with intangibles which is a separate discussion and I will be covering in another book.

There has been significant evolution in the way retail and retail outlets have changed. It is no longer limited to be a place to showcase and sell products. It is now a place that works on the aspects of

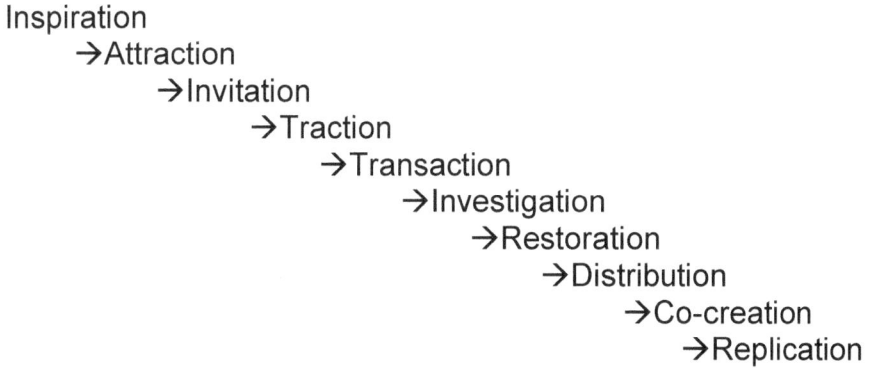

Inspiration
→Attraction
→Invitation
→Traction
→Transaction
→Investigation
→Restoration
→Distribution
→Co-creation
→Replication

Imagine taken on a journey that that is enjoyable and fulfilling. Buyers are part of the journey and not just lone bystanders to fulfil the transaction.

The other change that is happening around us is the increase in value of intangibles in business, though they are not part of discussions of this version however readers may like to explore that intellectual property, trademarks, patents, software, brand, process knowledge is creating greater value than the physical assets.

These intangibles can be recipes if you are in a restaurant business or work protocols which you may have turned it into art form incorporating different stages of customer journey. These can be your competitive advantage elements and can help you stand against competition with ease and stand the test of time. This can help you with your uniqueness or help you differentiate in the crowded marketplace.

While changes are occurring rapidly around us the businesses that are cognisant and adaptable to changes have managed to thrive in turbulence. The choices are strictly three - Adapt, innovate or be disrupted. Disruption and innovation are opposite sides of the coin. A change if happens to you beyond your control it is disruption, when you cause it to others is innovation.

I recall going to a few streets of Melbourne that were bustling with businesses and shoppers, now things of past. You can have only a limited number of cafe's or doctors that offer similar product or services be concentrated at a location. It then reaches a tipping point when it becomes non sustainable the blue oceans turn into read oceans and it becomes a dog eat dog world. Once may choose to make noise, to seek attention. When the guilds or associations form offering similar product or services, then they compete, some choose to differentiate, or others claim that they are better. Predatory action of pushing others out of the market and unethical games become rampant.

There are always right answers, but we always get caught in the game and assume, it is zero sum. Though there is no magic pill however the big mantra here is adaptability.

The other interesting change in the market is the platform economy. Aggregators of services and providers on an online platform. Some of the platforms have required significant investment initially to build a traction of buyers and sellers resulting into a self-perpetuating marketplace. These marketplaces say food service aggregators compete amongst themselves and missing out from one platform can be expensive for business at times. Settings own platform is expensive as well. Working with platforms may also mean that you share a significant chunk of the revenue with these platform providers eating into your profitability. How do you survive and thrive the game when revenue is steadily climbing, and profit is on rapid decline? For financial engineering this may be a Godsend however one may just be putting off the doomsday.

Companies like UberEATS, Menu Log, EASI are making money whilst many restaurants are going belly up. Tables are empty. There is a risk of backward integration when these highly vested in business move into ghost kitchens fulfilling the needs of the customers by offering products made in domestic kitchens leased to them. You no longer need floor space, tables chair to run a successful restaurant, you can run it from any kitchen. You just need to be able to offer consistently good food. If UberEATS starts partnering with all grandma's who can make delicious curries or minestrone, then will be the dawn of a new era. Businesses that run restaurant in the franchised environment run the risk as they are highly capitalised. There are answers but no silver bullet is hiding in this book. In fact, I strongly oppose any opinions and ideas you are being or have ever been sold where you are told that this magic pill will solve all your problems the chances are it won't, moving you from one wave of an idea to next.

The real method is to explore all the answers that are out there is like choosing your own colours from a palette to paint your own unique picture. You only choose what is relevant to you.

Think of these colours as your own data points or inputs. One observation you may have is people have started ordering food on these aggregation platforms. Does that mean the consumption is increased or just shifted or a bit of both? You may need to understand how this impact the type of business you are getting into in a geographic area. Perhaps you may need data or just drive around in the area or ask questions. Key is to not to assume anything but to question everything.

One may need to explore their business model, leadership and ability to make astute decisions. These decisions may be related to self, business, environment, competition, staff and other gamut of aspects. All visible positive change is not necessarily good if it harms the long-term customer and business value.

Sometimes you may offer fries to your customer as an add on, but sometimes you may have to just add it for free. When to make those choices is important. Can you have sustainable model? Because you are /are not offering the fries!

The challenge that franchise model presents is when market shifts, the business model is impacted. The model is dictated by franchisor and rapid changes can cause competing interests and conflicting priorities.

This book will surely take you on a journey and show you various aspects. it will not provide you all the answers that you may seek however it will share a perspective and once you see that perspective you will never be able to unsee it. It is expected to deepen your inquiry process, gain a better understanding on how to address the shift in market paradigm in retail.

Best

Sameer Babbar
BE, ME, MBA, GAICD

CHAPTER 1

Making right decisions, key to success

Business has evolved over generations. In his seminal book, *An Inquiry into the Nature and Causes of the Wealth of Nations* (1776), Adam Smith observed the process of producing drawing pins and noted that it can be broken down into 18 steps. He postulated the division of labour and its contribution to the wealth of society. Specialisation to become reality. He predicted that even the smallest of tasks would undergo differentiation.

Fast-forward to the present and we are living in that era. Take the example of McDonald's. The finest details are covered in their operations manual, which allows them to differentiate and standardise every step. Breaking elements of the business into simple steps and measuring each sub-step along the way to create differentiation, gain a clear competitive advantage, to win[1].

---

[1] Business can differentiate by understanding the process associated with creating

As differentiation[2] has increased, businesses are increasingly looking at creating new competitive elements to avoid facing extinction[3]. The ability to collect facts and information on the differentiating elements is now much easier due to the availability   of advanced technology and processes, that said requires discipline[4] and a clear intent. In the modern-day world, the ability to measure facts and to process vast amounts of underpinning data is increasing rapidly. Sometimes these facts are collated by those who may not be obvious subject-matter experts or authorities on the subject. You should ensure that these experts do not bring strong biases or personal preferences. Just as the author of the *Kama Sutra,* Vatsayana, actually lived a life of celibacy, there are many others who simply have an innate ability to describe facts without playing a part. You have every right to proceed with caution, however you should not discount these experts who can add their own perspective.

How we make decisions

Human lives are becoming complex, there is information and

---

awareness, the customer choosing the product, how it is delivered, what happens when it is delivered, installed, paid for, consumed, returned, repaired, serviced and disposed of. *Discovering New Points of Differentiation* by Ian MacMillan and Rita Gunther Mc-- Grath. *HBR*, July–August 1997

[2] Consumers today are faced with an explosion of choices. In this environment, distinctive product attributes are quickly copied by competitors, perceived by consumers to be minimal, or both. Those who fail to differentiate their product or service in the mind of the consumer won't stand a chance. Differentiate or Die: Survival in Our Era of Killer Competition by Jack Trout. Wiley Paperback, October 2001

[3] Blue Ocean Strategy by W. Chan Kim and Renee Mauborgne. HBR, October 2004

4 How to Measure Anything: Finding the Value of Intangibles in Business by Doug- las W. Hubbard. Wiley; (2nd edition) April 12, 2010

opinion overload, due to fuzziness it brings, an increasing number of decisions are constantly being made on gut feeling or emotions.

Recently, I was in discussion with a client who believed that we make either gut-feeling or fact-based decisions.

Our process of making decisions is considered dichotomous. It has become so natural in our decision-making process that now we have started seeing these two pillars as sacrosanct.

With a healthy balance of opinions with gut feeling and facts, we make well-rounded decisions this includes what we consume or buy.

"In God we trust; all others bring data," the famous saying by W. Edwards Deming, continues to be the anchor within business and industries that balances the decision-making process between faith and facts.

I would suggest that we now shift the gears and ensure that a more varied interplay of opinions is thrown into the mix to ensure decisions made are more likely to be well rounded.

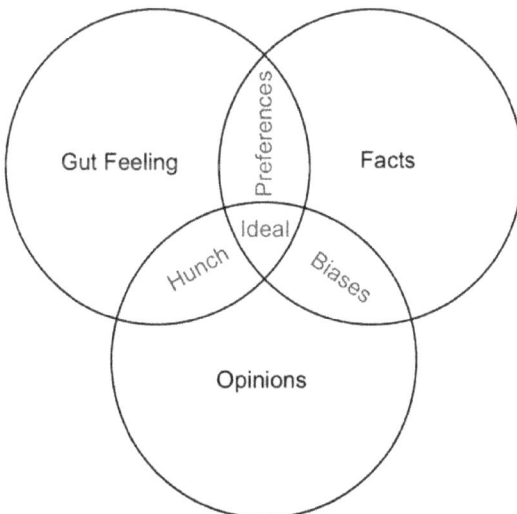

Many of those who have had success in business or life have the innate ability to use tacit knowledge and combine the dots to make decisions based on gut feeling. This, of course, is being done subconsciously.

No matter how confident we feel after collecting facts or relying on gut feeling, opinion from others can sway our decisions very rapidly. I am sure you may have come across a situation where you have carefully researched the market for, say, the next phone product, its features and operating system and found the right one that is just perfect for you and your friend told you it is iPhone X or nothing, that resulted in the purchase of brand-new iPhone X (or Samsung... but you get the picture).

When it comes to business, we collect data or facts and use the information to create insights. At times we selectively pick facts that match our hypothesis or opinions and let our biases play an important role. If you wanted to buy a Sony TV, you would try and find all the facts that reinforce your opinion. We are not trying to make the best decision here, but we are rather taking sides and proving our point. We need to know that our and others' cumulative biases can play a significant manipulative role here[5] , which, of course, can be taken advantage of.

If as a leader, should you choose to ignore facts and opinions, your decisions will always be challenged and considered autocratic. On the other hand, if you make pure fact-based decisions while ignoring (minority) opinions, you may end up

---

[5] Identifying the Biases Behind Your Bad Decisions by John Beshears and Frances- ca Gino. October 31, 2014

serving the preferences of a significant sub- group and thus cause unrest. As a business owner if you consider a serving a minority group niche strategy will help you.

We should never discount opinions offered by customers, advisors and many others who have our best interest in mind; however, they should be taken as opinions only and not necessarily as facts. If Henry Ford had taken on-board the opinions, market would always have suggested faster horses. We can let gut feeling and other people's opinions play a part, although they are nothing more than collective hunches. While they may point us in the right direction, as they lack facts they can as easily propel us in the wrong direction. This is akin to the blind leading the blind. Opinions require neither knowledge nor accountability.

In business or life, an ideal decision can be made when we rely on gut feeling, which is probably carved out of intensive or even generational expertise, supplemented with a wide range of facts which are then distilled down or peeled away like the layers of an onion to get to the core facts and augmented with opinions (which could also be perceptions). These can help us create leverage if we are observant.

This is akin to jumping from a height of 10 feet and knowing you will be safe due to the known facts that you are jumping into a pond and can swim. You may still need to rely on opinion that the pond still has water in it but basing your ability to swim on the number of books you have read is gut feeling.[6]

The most expensive decisions in bricks and

---

[6] Don't Trust Your Gut by Eric Bonabeau. HBR, May 2003

mortar businesses

A real estate decision is one of the most critical ones for any business. Besides labour costs, it is one of the most expensive elements. It can make or break the business or at least delay its profitability. It can make your on-the-road sales staff more efficient or cause them to burn out (if they have to reach out to customers who are far away from the business).

Two relevant questions any business has to constantly monitor are whether it is able to reach its target market on a consistent basis and whether the target market is able to locate it. If this is not happening for you, you run the risk of not being in business for long.

Businesses are becoming fiercely competitive and it is a constant struggle to be heard above the noise. Another question you as a business owner should constantly ask is whether the message from the business is compelling enough to make the target market hear it and then reach out for products or services.

A combination of the right message for the market and ensuring that either the market is able to reach you, or you are able to reach the market using the right mode of travel (or engaging with customers) is vital for success. All based on the premise that you have something of value that the universe is willing to pay.

Research suggests that less than 10% of bricks-and-mortar businesses demonstrate scalability, compete successfully, grow continually and genuinely add true value to the market. This only happens when the message, the market and the reach is all clear and relevant. Any business that has been operational over a period of time will show these traits.

If a business is not growing to keep pace with inflation, or better, chances are it is moving backwards. To distil it further, the following scenarios may apply to a business for the reasons suggested:

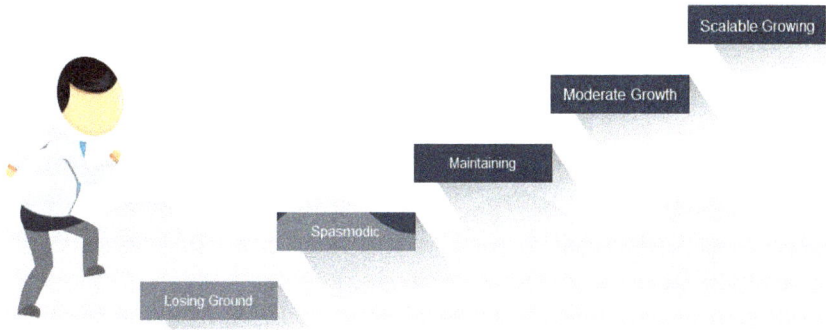

1. Losing ground

One has to figure out whether the ashes are those of a phoenix or just another chicken (akin to part #5 in the graph). A business that is losing ground is unsustainable. However, one has to dig deeper and find why the business is losing ground. It can be due to any of the following:

a. The business may be declining post-maturity as the competition may be trying to take away your business.

b. The business is unable to take off due to the business model changing, or a lack of customers.

c. You are trying to run the business as a hobby.

d. There is rapid disruption in the market.

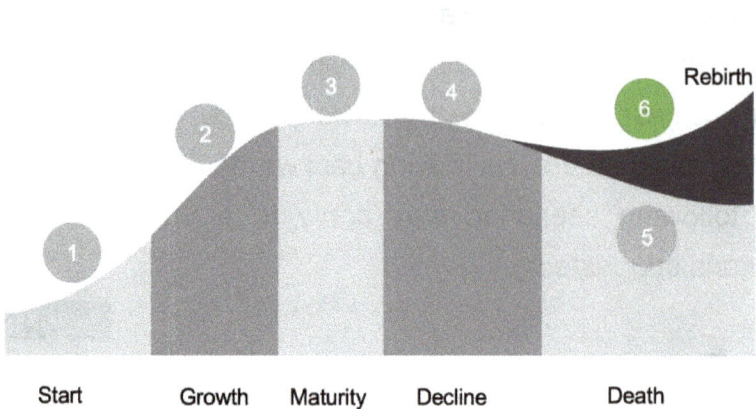

| Start | Growth | Maturity | Decline | Death |

This is the typical journey of a business; however, despite what the conventional wisdom may suggest, it does not necessarily go from left to right.

Inc.com suggests that 96% of businesses fail within 10 years. The Huffington Post suggests the figure is 95%, the Washington Post puts it at 90%and *HBS* Shikhar Ghosh (7 March 2011) at 70%. Irrespective of which study we accept, we can still say that the chances of any business surviving past 10 years is very low.

IBM has reincarnated itself many times on its journey and Kodak is coming back with blockchain.[7]

2. Spasmodic business

Like a sick person desperately needing treatment, a spasmodic business is one that is barely surviving because of

- fickle consumers who lack loyalty;

---

[7] https://www.reuters.com/article/us-crypto-currencies-eastman-kodak/kodak- blockchain-project-seeks-to-raise-50-million-in-token-offering-idUSKBN1IB1J7

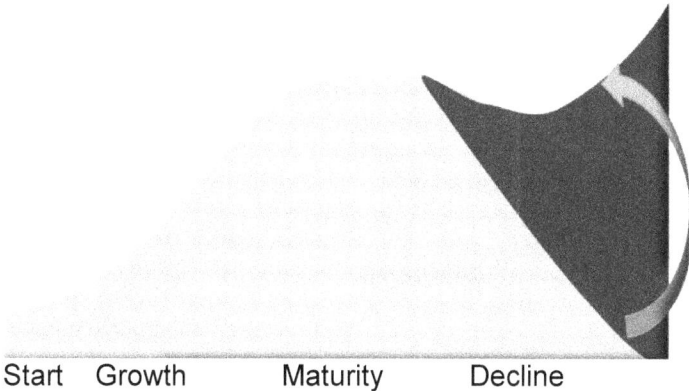

Start   Growth   Maturity   Decline

- intense competition that is eating up profits;

- a changing market (reducing in size or changing customer preferences);

- evolving business models (e.g., the business going online);

- changing capital or cost structure;

- minimal buyer expectations being raised;

- unions attempting to keep wages above what the market can support;

- the political landscape and tariffs;

- flipping industry standards that can take a product out of favour;

- poor management of the business or its finances;

- There are a lot of carcasses strewn across the Australian landscape[8]. These include

- Dick Smith's spectacular collapse on January 4, 2016[9];

---

[8] Reference HBR: *Curing the Addiction to Growth* by Marshall Fisher, Vishal Gaur and Herb Kleinberger. *HBR* (Jan–Feb 2017).

[9] https://www.afr.com/business/retail/appliances/what-killed-dick-smith-inside- the-dick-smith-collapse-20160908-grbgw6

- Radio Shack[10], perhaps because it could not keep up with the times.

There is obviously a desperate need for improvement, which may be achieved by some or all of the following factors:

- Operational improvements
- Enhancing real estate utilisation
- Analytics to track products and pricing (optimising)
- New product development
- Optimisation of staffing
- Capital utilisation
- Reviewing channel and licence fees
- Reviewing customer-facing policies (returns, credit cards)
- Subsidies by government: Sometimes it serves you well, but other times it can hasten your demise. For example, Holden started in 1948 in Australia. In the '50s it was the car of choice in every second household. Its sales peaked in 1963 with 166,274 cars sold. It was the top car in Australia for some time. However, over time it no longer remained the favourite.

  It needed government assistance to keep it going. It was also continually giving the impression that subsidy was its right as "every country subsidises its car industry"; however, when the policy changed, it was difficult for it to survive.

---

[10] https://www.forbes.com/sites/brianrashid/2017/04/08/the-complica- tions-that-lead-to-radioshack-declaring-bankruptcy-for-a-second-time-in-two-year-s/#1c24ce851303

3. Maintaining

This is a business that is sustaining itself but does not want to grow, as if it is permanently in a midlife crisis.

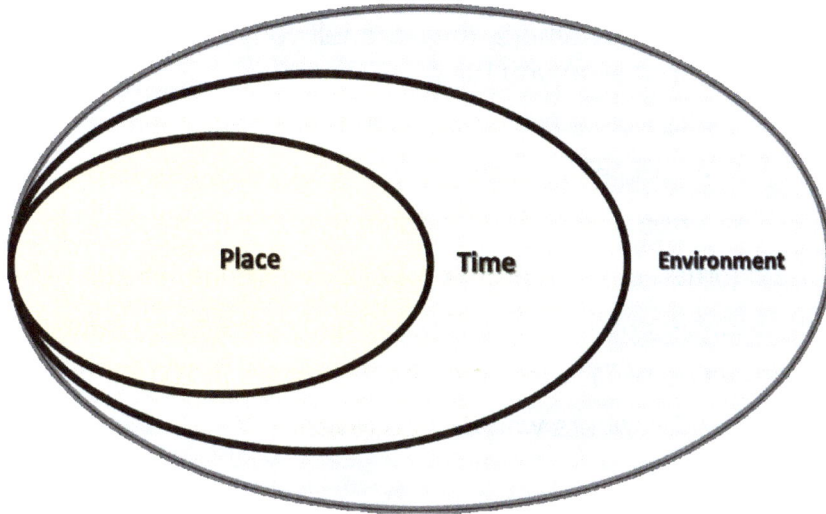

It is a business that is maintaining itself and not returning profits, but just the wages of all those involved in the business.

Things to look into with such a business will include the following:[11]

- Review the cost structure
- Review the market price
- Review offer alignment with market demand
- Ensure the business is optimally located to serve its target market
- Review inventory levels and work-in-progress levels
- Review payment terms (to suppliers and to clients)
- Review bad debts

[11] Value-Based Marketing: Marketing Strategies for Corporate Growth and Share- holder Value, 2nd edition, by Peter Doyle. ISBN: 978-0-470-77314-7. Oct 2008

- Review marketing effort and measure increase in-revenue post-marketing effort. You may need to look at customer acquisition cost per customer and customer life time value.
- Talk to customers, they can tell you how to make the most of what you have.
- Make bold strategic and long-term decisions

A classic example is Netflix (1997), which was founded by Reed Hastings and Marc Randolph to combat late fees. In 2003 it turned a 6.5 m profit on $272 m revenue. In 2011 DVD and streaming split, losing 800,000 subscribers and causing a drop-in value of 77% in 4 months. However, in 2018 it climbed to 120 m subscribers with $12 bn revenue.[12]

4. Moderate growth

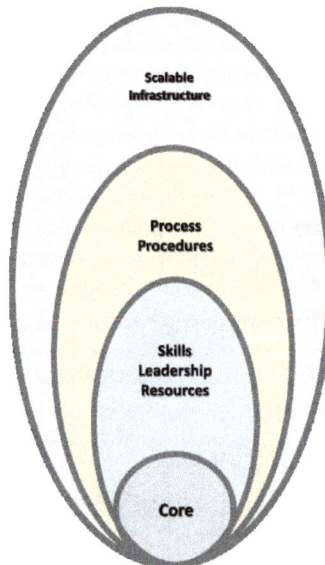

Scalable Infrastructure

Process Procedures

Skills Leadership Resources

Core

---

[12] Ref: Value Based Marketing: Peter Doyle

This is a business that is demonstrating moderate growth and increasing shareholder value, but in need of a catalyst. It is akin to a seedling needing more fertile ground, a better environment and some nurturing. In this scenario the core of the business is well established.

Important factors requiring the attention are as follows:

- **Core values**: These need to be well established to grow the business, though they are established at the onset and there is always some tweaking going on. *Unless the business is crystal clear on what it stands for, it will not amount to anything significant.* Until the business reaches moderate growth it is usually tinkering with products, technologies, ideas or services while the core is established. The solidification of the core will also identify what the business should do and what needs to be ignored. It is very easy to start experimenting with non-core activities that can throw the business/founders off track. Where the business is located is also at the core as it is important to find resources, technology and a competent staff marketand make an optimum choice as to what is likely to yield the best return based on available facts, opinions and gut feeling.

- **Skills, leadership and resources**: There should be multiple members in the leadership team to keep investment and business risk low. They also help in establishing the culture. It is at the stage when there are about 24 staff that the culture starts to become fully entrenched[13]. If the culture is not well entrenched, adding to the leadership team will also help in a two-pronged way, one by establishing a sounding board and the other by helping to bring business in through the door.

- **Process and procedures**: These help in streamlining tasks. Leverage and replicability in terms of products, services, platform, technology or any other aspect is what generates ongoing sustainable value and comparative advantage. Establishing the processes and procedures will thus help with the replicability of each aspect of the business. I was asked by a hairdresser who thought his job was difficult to be streamlined. Yet a bit of uncovering revealed that taking the booking over the phone, managing the diary, greeting the customer as they walked in, how the customer paid when the job was done, how the follow up-appointment was booked (or automated reminder sent to the customer to make a booking) turned a simple transaction into a repeat customer business with significantly higher customer lifetime value.

- **Scalable infrastructure:** It is important that in conjunction with replaceable procedures the focus should include how the entire infrastructure can become scalable. The advantage such thinking

---

[13] *HBR* : Four things to get right when starting a company, by Bruce Gibney and Ken Howery. May 09, 2012

considers replication of entire business model with or without involvement of investors (or franchisees)

5. Growth and/or potential.

When a business is demonstrating continuous growth, it deserves the need of cloning or leveraging as there are opportunities in the market that need immediate capitalisation. This is also required to prevent the competition from taking advantage of the opportunity to replicate the business model.

For a business that is showing potential for high growth and scalability in revenue the replicability can be of the whole business model. Such a business will need to have established the following:

- Standardisation of processes;
- A solid, focused and well-defined core;
- Business contingency and continuity planning
- The necessary skills and leadership to propagate the culture;
- Bootstrap investment and a franchise to scale the infrastructure and resources. Eventually your aim should be to create a monopoly business.[14]

Let us now take the example of McDonald's and Starbucks. No matter what part of the planet you are on, the stores in the

---

[14] Zero to One: Notes on Startups, or How to Build the Future by Peter Thiel and Blake Masters.

chain all look, feel, smelland taste the same.

Serve your market

Own the message, rule your market and control your reach.

For success in retail, it is critical that you pass the right message to the right market. The market can reach you with a mode of travel (e-travel/walk/ride/drive) or you can reach the market with genuine value and success is imminent. A simple addition of Uber delivery to a fast food restaurant added 20% to its revenue and the bottom line. This also freed up staff to enhance the experience of the dining-in experience.

The most expensive commitment for a business is the investment in lease or purchase of an asset at a location. Any bad decision can have undesirable consequences. Installing the business at the wrong location or for the wrong reasons (next to competition, cheap rental) without considering the spectrum of factors, can make its existence questionable.

Your location in the world; your customers in the catchment,

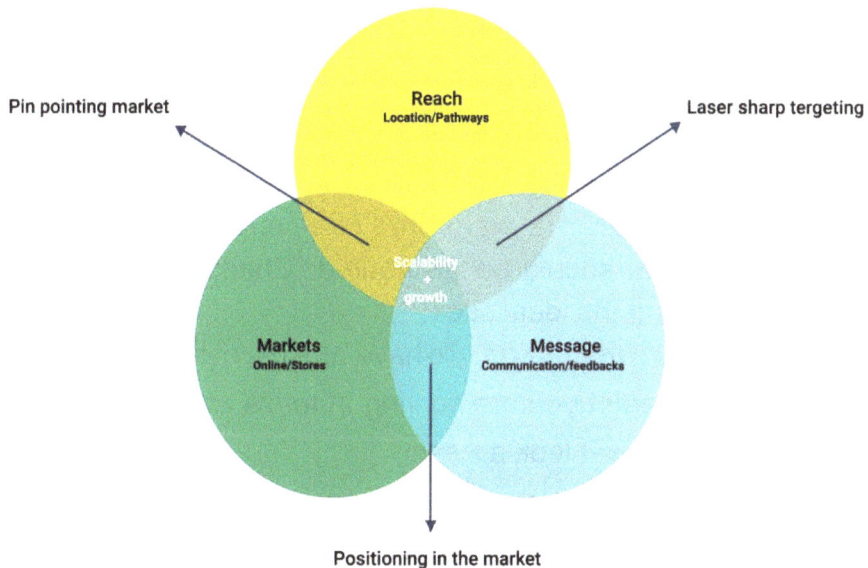

Pin pointing market

Laser sharp tergeting

Reach
Location/Pathways

Scalability
+
growth

Markets
Online/Stores

Message
Communication/feedbacks

Positioning in the market

either online or offline; your targeting of those customers; and your access to your customers, or customer visitation, are the elements that will help with the bottom line and business success.

Choosing the right location with insight will give you parameters that can help you grow your business in an unprecedented way and deal with the challenges posed by the onslaught of online sales, which has destroyed many bricks-and-mortar businesses. The physical interaction with your customer gives you opportunity to offer them an experience. It offers you an opportunity to understand them better and tailor your business to suit your customers' current, future and hidden needs.

This book relies heavily on a practical approach and meant to serve as a tool. As with any other tool, we would suggest you need to use your own judgment. There is no single best way to reach the outcome you desire; however, if you understand the drivers that underpin the success of your business you can easily scale your business.

I hope this book will inspire you and at the same time challenge you to dig deeper. This will guide you uncover the answer to the following questions as you move forward:

- **Store network planning:** To establish how your store network should be distributed. Chapter 5 talks about locating the ideal sites.
- **Sales forecasting:** To have an idea of sales based on the market you are serving in terms of demographics and market look alikes;
- **Cannibalisation:** Are you competing with yourself and leaving money on the table? Number of sections in the book talk about this. Chapter 9 is dedicated to this topic.
- **Demographics:** What is your market's sweet spot?
- **Spending trends:** What type of spender is your target market?
- **Acquisition due diligence:** Should you acquire a new business? Why? Where?
- **Catalogue distribution:** Where should you promote yourself and why? Chapter 7, discussion on loyalty card data suggests steps.
- **Sales force optimisation:** Should you send your

sales staff to where you have customers, or to where there are gaps in the market?

- **Benchmarking store opportunity versus output:** Should you benchmark multiple stores on revenue, or should you index them to opportunity their market presents?

- **Competitive intensity:** Is competition working for you or against you?

- **New products or services:** Should you new products or services be sold at premium price or low cost?

- **Logistics and supply-chain planning:** How can you reduce your logistics costs?

- **Media management:** What media should you use, where and why?

- **Point-of-sales tracking:** Do you need loyalty cards? Can you link them up with a point-of-sale system? And why?

- **Innovation opportunities:** Can you spot innovation opportunities in your business?

- **New business models:** Can you tap into some new business models and ideas?

- **Spot your own tribes based on lookalikes:** Can you spot the market lookalikes?

You may choose to read this book from cover to cover or section by section. Either ways you should use it as a guide or toolkit. It is not designed to give you answers. Its purpose is to point you in the direction where answers could be found. Each page you encounter may have a number of key points or ideas that you may consider incorporating in your business. I would therefore suggest that whatever section you read; you reflect on how it may apply to your business. Look at the questions included. If you are a consultant, then you may like to consider the value you can add to the business. Take notes, or email me to dig deeper into any aspects of information provided here (sbabbar@sameerbabbar.com)

CHAPTER 2

Thriving Environment for your business

There is a wide variety of types of stores from where a business is usually conducted following is a list though there can be variants hence the list is not exhaustive. The type of store will be based on the environment you are serving in[15].

Type of store

Arcade: A group of outlets in a walkway usually covered where the walkway takes advantage of foot traffic that cuts across two streets. Many historic arcades are now tourist attractions.

---

[15] Wikipedia contributors. Retail. Wikipedia, The Free Encyclopedia. September 17, 2019, 04:15 UTC. Available at:
https://en.wikipedia.org/w/index.php?title=Retail&oldid=916121711. Accessed September 18, 2019.

Image courtesy: pxhere.com

Anchor Store: A key tenant with a brand name and reputation that attracts a volume of shoppers to a precinct. Other shops in the precinct then leverage on this volume of shoppers.

Bazaar: This is how marketplaces are addressed in middle east, however in westernised connotations it may represent a temporary marketplace.

Image courtesy: pxhere.com

Boutique: Usually a small sized store focussing on a niche range of goods or products.

Image courtesy: pxhere.com

Category killer: A store that can kill a particular category for other retailers. Toys "R" Us (Toys: while it lasted), Bunnings (hardware, DIY, outdoor, gardening) Officeworks (stationery, home office, furniture). Stores like this offer an extensive range of products at an extremely low price and all under one roof. This makes it extremely difficult for smaller stores to compete.

Chain store: A series of stores owned by the same company or some owned and some franchised selling the same or similar products. Chain stores benefit from economies of scale (volume purchase, leading to lower purchase cost which can be appropriated by the chain or its customers) and scope (central warehousing, marketing, promotion, administration, transportation, design, etc.).

Concept store: The purpose of these stores is usually to offer an experience to customers; hence they focus on limited range of products or brand. Apple and Godiva fall into this category.

Co-operative store: A joint venture owned and operated by consumers to meet their social, economic, community and cultural needs.

Consignment shop: One can place an item in a store and if it sells the shop owners gives the person a percent of sale price. The advantage of selling an item this way is that the established shop gives the item exposure to more potential buyers.

Convenience store: Limited item store allowing quick transactions. Usually opening longer hours found in neighbourhoods or petrol stations

Department store: Stores that hinge on customer service. These stores offer a wide range of goods at moderate prices.

Destination store: A destination store is one that customers will initiate a trip specifically to visit, sometimes travelling great distances.

Discount store: Competing mainly on price a discount store offers a wide range of products and services.

E-tailer: Business that offers an online store front where a prospective customer can browse and order products and then the merchandise is delivered to customer.

General merchandise retailer: A retailer who stocks a wide variety of products in considerable depth. The types of product offerings vary across this category. Department stores, convenience stores, hypermarkets and warehouse clubs are all examples of general merchandise retailers.

Give-away shop: As the name suggests this shop provides goods for free. Sometimes customers are expected to pay what they can afford.

Hawker: It is usually a mobile vendor that operates in streets squares or public places. Hawkers or street vendors leverage areas with high foot traffic or impulsive purchase decisions. Hawkers are a relatively common sight across Asia.

Photo by *Linh Pham* on *Unsplash*

Hypermarket: large store providing variety and volumes of exclusive products at low margins. They have high floor area say over 20000m2.

General store: Store focusses on supplying the needs of a local community in outback or rural areas with low population densities (instead of focussing on a range of goods or products). Sometimes these general stores are very sparsely located. The general store carries a very broad range of products– from foodstuffs and pharmaceuticals through to hardware and fuel. Further, a general store may provide essential services including postal, banking and news agency and may operate as an agent for farm equipment and stock-food suppliers. These may be adjoining a pub or diner and together they may also meet the social and dining needs of the community.

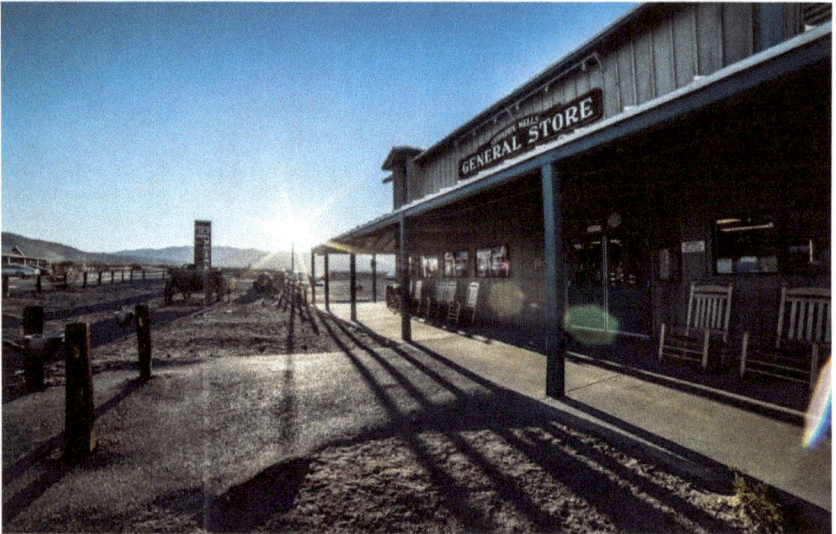

Photo by *Chor Tsang on Unsplash*

Mall: Usually when we group a number of retail shops in a single building or outlet. This can be on a single or multiple level. These are very complex and run by central management or marketing authority. The purpose of this central authority is to ensure the mall attracts the right type of retailer and has the appropriate retail mix.

Mom-and-pop store: It takes the name as it is usually owned and operated by an individual or family. The focus is to sell limited set of products, more often the owners are well intertwined in the social fabric of the area.

Pop-up store: When there is a cheap rental available between a tenant moving out and new one coming in or a space leased during festive season during enhanced foot traffic, temporary retail opens up for a short duration to sell a niche set of products or meeting demand for special occasion. During this occasion significant impulse buying activity takes place. The impulse also is enhanced should the products exhibit a greater sense of novelty. Hence greater chance of success.

Retail market: A place for retail sales of all products, packed and unpacked. If you are in middle east a marketplace of this kind is usually referred to as souq.

Market Square: An area where set of businesses set up stalls and buyers browse the stores. This kind of market is very ancient and countless such markets are still in operation around the whole world.

Speciality store: A focussed store specialising in specific merchandise, such as toys, footwear, or clothing, or on a target audience, such as children, tourists, or plus-size women. Such stores, regardless of size, tend to have a greater depth of specialist stock than general stores and generally offer specialist product knowledge that is valued by the consumer. Customers visiting such speciality store are not

27

usually price sensitive. Brand image, selection choice and purchasing assistance are seen as more important in making purchase decision at such stores.

Supermarket: A self-service store containing mainly grocery and limited-range products on non-food items with a Hi-Lo (starting from high then moving to low when the demand falls, or the quality products have been cherry picked by customers) or EDLP (Every day low price) pricing.

Variety store: An extremely low-cost goods store with a vast array of products sometimes the quality of the items is not of concern for the vendor.

Vending machine: Leveraging automation and eliminating human intervention, for selling, customers drop the money in the machine, make a selection which then dispenses the customer's selection. It is a self-service option. Though sometimes one may need to call a phone number in case of faults. These machines can take anything from a no-frills to a high- end approach.

A vending machine in Japan – Image courtesy pxhere.com

Warehouse club: A club or a membership-based retailer business that usually sells a wide variety of merchandise, in which customers may buy large, wholesale quantities of the store's products. This makes these clubs attractive to both bargain hunters and small business owners. The stores operate in a no-frills format that helps them to keep prices low. Further customers may be required to pay annual membership fees in order to shop there. A typical example in this category is Costco.

Warehouse store: A group of retailers housed in a warehouse who offer low-cost, often high-quantity, goods with minimal services. Goods are piled on pallets or steel shelves.

Reach between business and customers

Owning or leasing a physical location is perhaps one of the key expenses for any business that requires a physical location, unless you are an online store selling digital products (in this case reaching your customers via reliable delivery mechanism or customers reaching your online store in a noisy world is important).

The overheads in many cases may be high and if the traffic that leads to transactions does not prevail in the area then the return on investment may be poor (or prospects who use browse your online store without buying or abandoning site). You should also be mindful of the traffic that comes in-store to explore the product and then price-match to find the cheapest product online, or the traffic that leads to pilferage. Some stores offer that they can match any advertised physical store price and further discount it by 10% (that way they prices can still be kept high and for price sensitive shoppers they can discount it without losing a single customer)

You may want to experiment with the option of taking the store to the customer's doorstep. This can be done physically yourself or by using a third party that takes you online. Uber eats have redefined this paradigm for number of businesses.

Factors that influence business success

It is important to understand what success[16] is and what causes it at a location. This also needs clarity on the nature and purpose of business one is in. There is a massive list of factors that impact the business at a location. The influence of the factors is correlated with revenue and cost to understand the drivers and detractors. This process also helps to identify irrelevant factors that really do not affect the outcome and may be wasteful to focus energy on.

Just to take an example, we can't say with certainty whether McDonald's offers the best burgers, but they certainly sell lots of them from their 37,000 plus stores around the globe. Likewise, Starbucks may not offer the best coffee in the world, but they sell lots of it from more than 27,000 plus stores.

That said McDonald's is actually in the real estate business; The revenue from flipping burgers allows the franchisees to pay them the rent.

Bunnings is a consulting company that where consultants help identify what products will solve a customer's problems. Though it may come across differently to the market.

Sometimes it may not be evident what business one may be in; it is based on the core is that drives business and impacts the bottom line (or triple bottom line). It may not be evident, and introspection may be required. The following are some of the factors you may need to consider when planning your business:

---

[16] I recommend the concept "People, planet and profit" to describe the triple bottom line and the goal of sustainability, by **John Elkington** in 1994

Factors based on trade area or catchment

You may need to consider the factors that may be relevant for you from the following list.

- **Current Potential:** The vested potential in the market you intend to serve now
- **Demographics:** What are the current demographics? How it is shifting? Is it seasonal? Do people travel to this area to work?
- **Market size:** How big is the market? Is it enough to sustain your business? Is it sustainable if you account for competition?
- **Population:** Is the population large enough to grow your business into? Is it possible to add new products or services to cater to the population?
- **Catchment area:** How far are people willing to travel to come to seek your offerings? Are you able to reach out to them within an area?
- **Purchasing power:** Is the market able to afford the products or services you have on offer?
- **Future potential:** Is the market likely to grow in the long run, or is it declining? Is the level of affluence on the rise?
- **Competition quality (degree and number):** Is the competition increasing or declining?

Factors based on site where business is located.

- **Configuration:** What is the layout? Is the shop in the front or the back? Far away from parking or next to it?
- **Business in the neighbourhood:** What is the type of

business that prevails in the area? Does it bring in traffic? Does this cater to a specific niche in the market? Does that street stand for a range of goods sold (diamond merchants if fifth avenue New York or Gold Market in Dubai)?

- **Accessibility:** Is it easy to get in and get out of the area? Does it attract the physically or visually impaired to shop in the area?

- **Visibility:** Is the business physically visible, or do you only find it once you get there? How do people find the place? Is the banner large enough to be visible from a distance? Some businesses like to play games with the banner. Note the picture below and think about what your perception of the business is the first time you read it; then read it again carefully.

- **Agglomeration effect:** When complementary

businesses are co-located, it often helps to attract more suppliers and customers in the area. Although co-location results in competition, which drives prices lower, the overall effect helps to attract a wider customer base. It also offers economies of scale and rapid building of network effects (more buyers bring more sellers and vice versa causing exponential growth). As more businesses become co-located, the availability of labour builds up over time, although this may drive the asset prices up and lead to high-density areas where ingress and egress becomes a challenge over time.

- **Foot traffic:** This is among the best measures of success in the event of an impulsive purchase.
- **Anchoring:** Based on the past offering, businesses like McDonald's attempt to build expectation relying on your past purchases. You are going on a long drive and then you see Golden Arches. Anticipation builds up and you may be compelled by your family or kids to stop there (a toy shop that also has food). It's not necessarily about quality of food you are likely to get – it's about predictability of standards all the times.

Factors based on what happens in Business/Store

- **Gender/Age:** The gender and age of the person making the purchase and person providing the service. In case of a client after sifting through lot of data we identified that old women who were the key influencers talked to older salesmen who closed the sale with ease while talking about kids and grandkids.

This in turn helped them with their recruitment strategy.

- **Interest:** They may have an interest in buying a product or service. You may also need to understand what stage of the purchase journey they are at.

- **Key purchase criteria:** They may be constrained by some preferences, or they may have purchase priorities. Sometimes it is price; sometimes it is features. You need to figure out what those triggers are.

- **Influences:** Who influences the purchase? They may be buying, but the decision about the purchase may not be theirs. As in the above paragraph, we found that grandmothers were the main influencers in the purchase of carpets.

- **Value sought:** What is it that the customers seek that they attribute to as value.

- **Captive customers:** A higher number of captive customers may lead to a higher reference base if customers are pleased with the products or services.

- **Experience/skill of staff:** Staff with poor experience may show the product and leave the decision to the customer. Staff with rich experience may be able to uncover the customer's needs better, to help them make a better purchase decision, leading to high satisfaction levels besides closing the sale.

- **Loyalty of customers:** A loyal customer base leads to a higher frequency of purchases and over time the customer lifetime value increases.

- **Size of store:** The floor area on which customers can move around and see the items stocked.

- **One-stop shop:** Having a one-stop shop can help customers come to a destination where their needs can be fulfilled. If only some of the needs of customers are fulfilled, then the customers may shop around at other locations. This may lead to greater opportunities of price matching and feature comparison, hence diminished value captured by your business.

- **Configuration:** Store configuration and visibility impact on purchase decisions. Dark corners with diminished lighting lead to a feeling of insecurity. It is well known that supermarkets stock milk in the back corner to ensure that you are paraded through the aisles to lead you to make some collateral impulsive purchase decisions.

- **Convenience:** This helps customers make low-value decisions. When the customer runs out of milk they can go to the nearest outlet. Sometimes customers are time-sensitive more than price-sensitive when they are in the store.

- **Longevity of the store:** Some stores act as a landmark if they have been around for a long time. They become part of the local culture. If you remember going to an ice cream store after dinner while growing up, chances are your kids will be introduced to it and such purchases may transcend generations.

- **Staff morale/experience:** Staff with positive morale will serve customers better and try to make their purchasing experience more enjoyable. They will be helpful and demonstrate value to customers. Negative morale amongst staff can lead to pushy sales and closing techniques being used. This may work in the short term but will damage the business in the long run. Such staff may move on, but the scars of their bad behaviour will be carried by your business for a long time. To sell to the market in any area or part of the world you need a team of competent staff who can understand the customer linguistically and behaviourally. That means availability of local staff (the customer-facing ones) is vital. Blackburn Cellars a bottle shop in Melbourne started giving complimentary lemons to its customers on the weekend to help them avoid making a trip to supermarket. It was a small step towards exceptional customer service however it laid the foundations to stock items for cocktails which is now part of their rapidly growing components of business.

- **Market awareness:** How strong is your brand? How quickly can your prospects recall it? How has the history of their experience with you and your brand been? I recall a businessman who would disguise himself as a customer and ask strangers and passers-by where his shop was. The ones who knew would point him in the right direction, while others would wonder, plead ignorance and then later on try and figure it out on their own to fulfil their curiosity. The one's who recognised him got a voucher. The strategy worked.

- **Access to the site:** Sometimes you have to ensure that access to the site is easy. With an exception of adult stores have constrained access to their site, to prevent under- 18 walk-ins and social taboos.

- **Appearance/Aesthetics:** It is expected that the shop front should look inviting. An unhygienic or dirty environment can repel a segment of customers.
- **Rent:** High rent in an area can make a business untenable, especially in malls. Low rents may lead to profit, but they may not offer a critical mass of customers to make the business viable. You should always try and study the volume and type of traffic in

conjunction with the rent of the place.

- **Technology used:** In an online or a physical store, the technology used can enhance or degrade the customer experience. For instance, a one-click checkout, if customer details are available, will reduce purchase friction.

- **Exposure:** This includes the frontage, signage and the type of traffic flowing through in the vicinity that helps with awareness and recall.

- **Traffic or congestion:** Is the traffic productive for business, or merely road congestion. If it is congested that might be a boon for hawkers (in some parts of the world).

- **Truck size (for turning radius and accessibility):** In narrow
lanes, large trucks cannot get in and turn, so modes of delivery are required that make it feasible to get in and out quickly. Sometimes in business hubs, such shopfronts are for negotiation, sampling and retail. Wholesale and deliveries usually take place from their delivery centres.

- **Inside the curve:** The visibility of the shop is poor if it is inside the curve. If the traffic on the street moves at a reasonable speed, the chances are that customers may miss the shop. On the contrary, if it is on the inside curve and there is a lot of foot traffic, the chances are that it will never go unspotted.

- **One-way street:** Having a shop on a one-way road simply means that if you have missed it then you have to take the full circle around a block or two to arrive at the same spot. If there are alternatives available, customers are likely to switch.

- **Turning direction in your country:** This leads to traffic friction. If you drive on the left-hand side of the road, then turning right may sometimes cause significant delays. If you run a delivery company, that will impact the overall fuel consumption and the number of deliveries you can make in a year. UPS for example decreased their fuel consumption by 10m gallons and delivered 350000 more packages by avoiding left turn in 2016 (in US where the traffic moves on the right-hand side of the road)

- **Parking design:** How easy it is to park and unpark (ingress and egress)? How safe do you feel the parking is? Thefts in the parking area hinder shopping decisions. Sometimes the parking, particularly if free, is consumed by nearby residents within the area, which leads to less parking available for genuine buyers. Time limits and cost of parking (if reasonably enforced) can reduce such issues. Graffiti and smoking in car parks may be seen as unsafe by many buyers. Well-lit car park in the night gives a sense of security.

- **Activities:** Play areas do help attract and retain customers, as do activities such as kids' face painting.

The scope of your business

As a business, you can choose the scope within which you

41

want to play you can play a big game or stay a small business. In other terms, you can be a small fish in a big pond or big fish in a small pond. You can stay local and serve the local market, or aim to grow global (depending on how opportunity presents itself and is capitalised - you should be mindful of cultural fit, opportunity, demand, timing, etc.) At times we find that reasons for business expansion are often more emotional or political than pragmatic.

Your business may start as a corner store. The success or failure of the business will depend on market demand for the products or services offered (at a given point in time); the market opportunity – whether it is expanding or diminishing (opportunity trend); and the cultural fit of what is being offered and what the expectation is. Hofstede[17] has provided extensive information on the topic. Many businesses have suffered because the cultural fit was poor. An example of this was MacDonald's attempt in selling beef burgers in India. In September 2012, they faced a tremendous challenge when trying to sell beef in Katra in Jammu and Kashmir State and Amritsar, due to religious protests. Similarly, in April 2014 McDonald's faced an investigation, as the food served was claimed to be not halal. Though there was a demand and the size of opportunity was stable, cultural fit with the market was very poor and as a result it did not do well until it had tailored its offerings to what the market would accept.

---

[17] The Hofstede model – Applications to global branding and advertising strategy and research, by Marieke de Mooij and Geert Hofstede. International Journal of Advertising, 29(1), pp. 85–110, 2010 Advertising Association, Published by Warc, www.warc.com www.warc.com. doi: 10.2501/S026504870920104X.

There is also a very interesting research TED[18] talk on the timing of the offering. Trends and tastes keep changing in the market and so do preferences. For any given business to do well, it is essential that the timing is right.

The business Scope Model

A typical business scope in a market looks like the following:

[18] The single biggest reason why startups succeed, by Bill Gross
https://www.ted.com/talks/bill_gross_the_single_biggest_reason_why_startups_suc
ceed?language=en

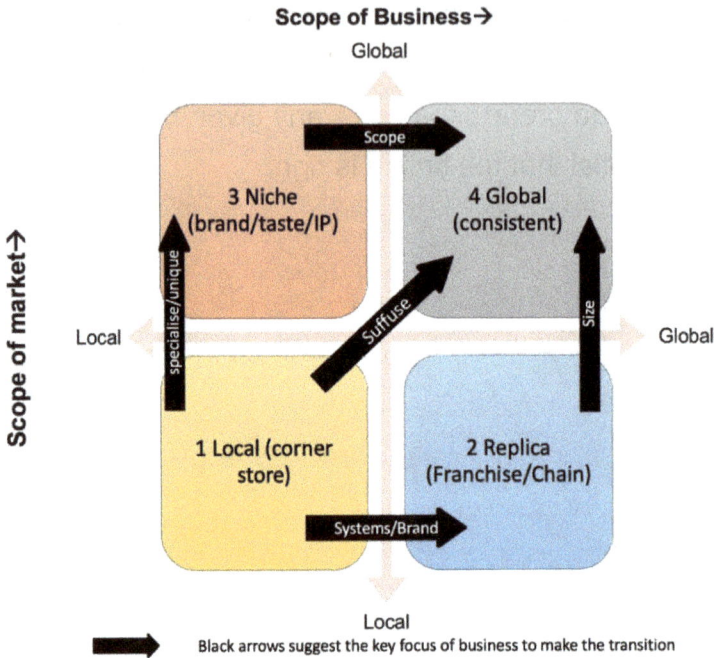

Black arrows suggest the key focus of business to make the transition

1. The corner store

A typical corner store is what caters to the needs of the ones living in the immediate proximity. Stores in this case cater to the needs of those living in the catchment area of the store. A small fraction of the customers may include passing traffic. Hence in this case it meets the well-defined needs of which are not currently being met within the known and identified geographic, demographic and psychographic.

The important thing to keep in mind here is how far the customers are willing to travel to get to the store, are they driving, biking or walking (or in some cases you may need to consider if they are flying in).

As a store becomes super successful in a geographic area

attempting to meet the unmet needs of people, the category of services or product become well *defined*. As soon as this happens a lot of me-too stores open up trying to replicate and take advantage of the business model and *deliver* the offering to same set of customers *developing* their own variants. A simple example of this could be a grocery store or a cafe. Once it is successful and suddenly gets swamped with customers, it gives ideas to others and suddenly more stores offering similar product and services start opening in that area, thus quickly saturating the market which becomes *competitive*. This happens in online space as well hence a number of providers keep the market confused about the group of products or services they offer. A classic example is Google's alphabet or Amazon. It is extremely difficult to exactly define the list of products or services they have on offer at any given point in time.

This makes it very difficult to understand or replicate their business strategy.

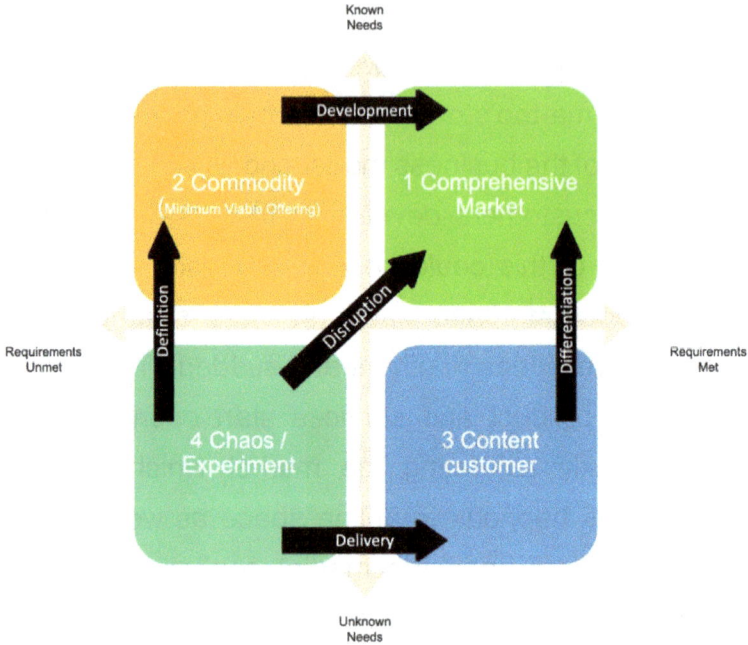

Babbar's opportunity exploitation matrix

Sometimes the competitive intensity grows to the point that the businesses start cannibalising each other vying for the same customers within the same market hence the revenue and thereby profitability declines. This movement from chaos to clarity where the offerings get well *defined* to become a *commodity* in the market for opportunity exploitation is defined in the **Opportunity Exploitation Matrix**. For well-defined needs that can be met by existing providers, addition of new provider can add to competition in the market.

If the purpose is to stay a corner store, then your aim should be to become the best corner store there is and as the competition starts copying you your aim should be to keep offering added value to customers and differentiate your products and services to stand out.

2. The replica store

Replica stores can be clones of themselves. Chain stores or franchised stores fall into this category.

The intellectual property, infrastructure elements, business model, processes etc. of the business is carefully replicated to ensure that the offering and brand is translated across all the stores. They all have a similar look, feel, music, artefacts and even smell. There is a great focus on *systems* and *branding* to ensure replication.

In cases where the stores are franchised, there is an exchange of license fees from franchisee to franchisor.

The model helps the franchisee with early cashflows and returns on investment leveraging on the brand, processes and knowhow, while the franchisor gets an investment and an ongoing fee with an increase in market penetration and enhanced brand perception. Extending further, it offers economy of scale and scope, which helps to improve the bottom line as new stores are added to the network.

For a franchisor and franchisee understanding, measuring and monitoring the following measures is crucial:

- **Market penetration**: The greater the relevant penetration,

  the better it is for a business. On the surface higher penetration may appear good for a business, however it may indicate overinvestment in infrastructure. Management in a large international chain in Australia claimed that they have great market penetration and irrespective of where they open the store the business is doing very well. What we uncovered that though they are extremely successful they continue to over invest in infrastructure and installing the stores very close to each other which is not necessary.

Market gaps: No matter how close your stores are there will always be gaps in the market. Not everyone may buy your product there can be different market preferences, your offering may respond to different age segment, your opening hours may have varying alignment with your target market segments, your brand recognition may vary from area to area, convenience or customer proximity may also vary. You should worry about gaps only if you are missing out on a lucrative market that is well within your catchment.

Territory (if franchised): It can be a contentious area between franchisor and franchisee if the franchisor has been over- enthusiastic about the market potential. At the same time, it can be frustrating and a cause of agony if the market conditions become adverse. It is advisable to ensure transparency and a relationship that takes a long-term perspective.

Cannibalisation among stores: If stores are close by, some cannibalisation is inevitable. Some cannibalisation can be deliberate to thwart competition in a lucrative territory.by keeping penetration at high levels.

Competitive intensity: Due to increased competitive intensity, individual profits fall, but it leads to expansion of the market. A physical area attracts customers from a greater distance away and leads to the formation of associations and guilds to preserve profits.

The shape of the town: How a town is laid out can have a significant effect on the business as it impacts access, travel times and how population settles.

It is also important to understand the rationale in the following as a group

The logic of distribution of shops: Is there a logic or pattern to the way in which shops are located (close to schools, close to cinemas/theatres, left or right side of street when going to work or coming from work as this can impact flow of traffic and as a result business)?

Logistics of staff and supply: staff are travelling a great distance to get to work, staff located optimally to serve the territory, supply chain is optimal with easy ingress and egress of products from suppliers

Attractors and detractors of business: elements that will pull business towards or push business away

Franchise reports with a view to selling: putting your best and honest view regarding a business for a potential buyer. Window dressing for short term gains is not unheard of however I will strongly discourage it as it will impact your long-term reputation.

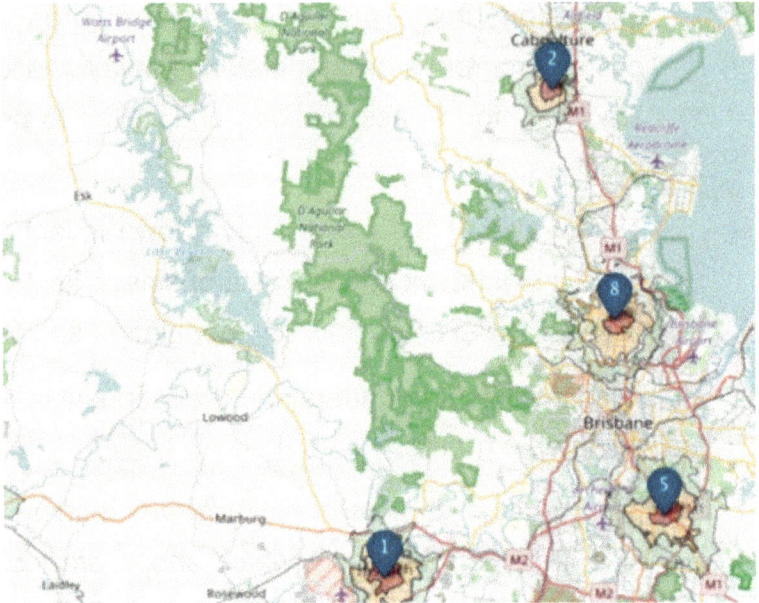

Market penetration: for a franchise group is the total penetration including franchisor- and franchisee-owned stores. Each store has its own penetration and local level; however, as a group it may still have penetration locally for each entity as it may span across state, regional, national boundaries and may exist as a multinational. Further complexities might be added such as listing on stock exchanges. (For example, Domino's pizza is listed in the ASX.) Which suggests that you should understand penetration of your or competing business at multiple levels

To create higher penetration for business which extends to wide geographic, political and cultural area you need to consider

- mass localisation (local taste, religious, cultural

or professional preferences);

- cultural issues when extending the national or regional boundaries (Geert Hofstede Country Comparison Tool: https://www.hofstede-insights.com/product/compare-countries/)
  such as McDonald's selling beef burgers in India was opposed strongly by religious and political groups as it did not align itself with the ethos.

Missing Penetration: There can be gaps in the market for a franchise group. A prudent question any business needs to ask is whether these gaps are due to

1. a lack of sufficient potential;
2. the inability of business to scale up; or
3. ignorance of the sufficient potential that exists.

The franchise system works best in Scenario 1. However, for scenario 3, in-depth analysis is needed on an ongoing basis; even more so that it is difficult to identify whether there is a true lack of potential, or unrealised potential due to lack of knowledge or action on behalf of the group owners.

A textbook case here in Australia was observed when a new chain "Wood Frog Bakery" started opening stores close to the incumbent "Bakers Delight", it included incumbent's flagship store. Although they both sell bakery products, they both target a slightly different preference group in the market. As the value proposition is good and differentiation is great, both bakeries are well placed.

That said, Masters, with a strategy similar to that of Bunnings, started opening home improvement stores in the vicinity. However unlike how it seemed on the surface, Bunnings operated as a free consultancy company that provided information on products that helped the consumer solve a problem, whereas Masters focused more on the products themselves and saw value to the customer more as a result of product and price, rather than solving the client's problems, in contrast to Bunnings. As a result, Masters was unable to replace the incumbent, besides low price and some differentiation it was unable to offer genuine value to buyers. It was unable to translate that in high transaction numbers and as a result was unsuccessful.

Exclusivity on Market Penetration: In the franchisor and franchisee relationship, the franchisee likes to have some form of rights to an area that comes with the territory, as it gives both the franchisor and a franchisee a level of confidence that the business will go quite well.

Not compromised by franchisees or franchisers, it is actually an intent from the franchisor to expand its business in an area, whilst the franchisee gets an exclusive right to work in an area. It gives a franchisee an exclusive right of refusal, that the franchisor will not provide a right to business to anyone else in that area. These rights may be given on a number of factors, such as suburb or state national boundary. So, these can be exclusive within a territory, or on first right of refusal; or, if there is any other business that comes on sale, the existing franchisee could have a right to buy that. Confusion on territorial rights is a common cause of dispute between franchisors and franchisees.

Penetration guzzler - Cannibalisation

Similar businesses that are in close proximity may end up sharing the same customers and when businesses share the same customers, they can be some cannibalisation, with inevitable loss of revenue.

Just to take an example, if you gain an advantage of just 20% of customers because you are managing cannibalisation very well and get them to come 20% more often, that simply means that you get 40% uplift in business revenue and that is significant.

To manage cannibalisation, it will help to understand the law of gravitation; suggesting all being equal, customers prefer to shop in the closer proximity. That said, the other attractions in that area where the business is located will impact on how far the customers are willing to travel. If customers are willing to travel a great distance because of the large number of attractions close to the business, the relevance of cannibalisation is diminished as the catchment area of business is enlarged.

The attached diagram a typical in distribution of customers suggests that given a store location, the most frequent customers come from a nearby location, whereas infrequent customers come from either nearby or far away locations. We can make valuable inferences if we have customer loyalty data (to link purchase to the geographic area of origin of those customers)

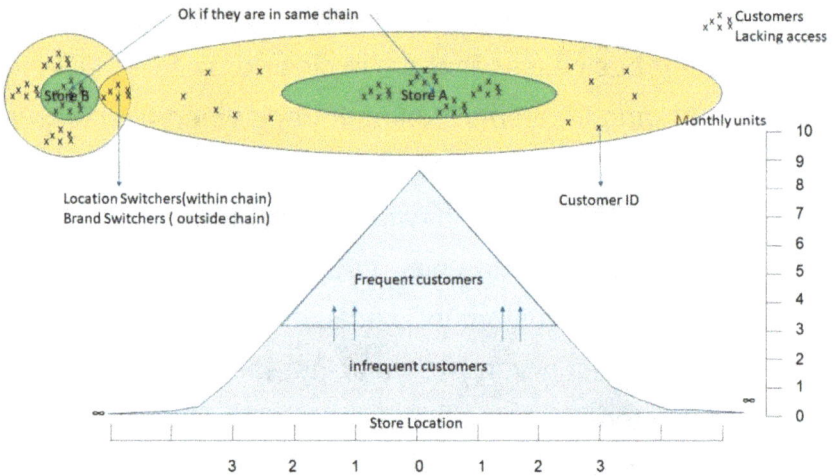

Using loyalty card data (or any identifiable information about customers) we can plot the distance the customers are coming from with respect to the store location. The diagram shows the frequency distribution of customers with respect to distance from the store.

Now let's take two locations, store location A and store location B; a particular customer can be living in close proximity to location A but might be going to shop at location B as they prefer shopping within the same group or chain. It's good for the business. However, if the customer switches their preferred chain, that is a measure of customer promiscuity.

Hence. Customers can fall into different categories. They can be location switchers within the same chain stores, or they could be promiscuous to the brand.

More lucrative the opportunity, the higher the competition. As competitive intensity grows, it continues to go beyond sustainable levels, at which point one of the two things, or possibly both (assuming everything else stays the same), can happen:

- The underperforming business has to exit the market (or be acquired).
- Customers start coming from (or business reaches out to) nearby areas due to increased choice.

As an example, when there are lots of cafés in a given area, the competitive intensity mounts up, some cafés start offering Wi-Fi, newspapers and some other facilities to attract the customers and so get them to increase their consumption by retaining them for a longer period. In Melbourne, a laundromat offers free Wi-Fi, massage chair, TV, tea, coffee and newspapers to differentiate while thwarting competitive intensity. The bar just got raised.

Patterns and strategies of market penetration

Human dependence on water has resulted in the establishment of cities around drinking water, irrigation channels, or transportation routes. Overlay that with the geography of an area and we start seeing the patterns of how the shape of the cities emerged. Further existing transportation have their routes dictated also the pattern of establishment shops within those cities from among the following patterns:

- Linear, along a route or river

Distribution of shops along a river: Image Courtesy: pxhere.com

- Ribbon, along the route
- Star-shaped
- Serpentine
- Fishbone

How the town is established will help work out the hubs and spokes that may impact the business. Most successful chain stores or franchise stores follow some logic in building their network. This may include a number of strategies with key objectives to reach the maximum penetration for economic returns in the most cost-effective manner.

Some strategies can be among the following;

- Cloning another network
- Staying far away from the competition
- Staying very close to competitors and giving options to existing customers
- Making it extremely difficult to define their category and the niche they play in so that it's extremely difficult for a competitor to replicate the strategy.

For example, McDonald's is more likely to be found near schools or high-volume road traffic.

Penetration Influencer: Attractors and detractors

Attractors and detractors bring or take away opportunity from an area respectively; attractors pull in traffic and detractors push them away. They can be general in nature or may impact a specific type of business.

Traffic is also impacted when similar types of businesses are close by. For example, if there are eateries on a given street, people chose that street to dine because they want to go and eat a particular type of food that that street may be popular for. People don't pick the shop, but they pick the street.

3. Niche business-
Leveraging uniqueness

Sometimes, it is preferable to create the barriers by using a secret sauce or recipe that customers can get hooked that is difficult to replicate. An example in this case would be the Coca-Cola recipe, which is a closely guarded secret. Patents and trademarks create barriers to entry. It serves as a safeguard that the incumbent's business will continue for a reasonable period of time. However, information about patents and trademarks is publicly available, which creates the risk of copycats and counterfeiters.

Sometimes it is the replicability of the taste that helps in differentiating a business.

Sometimes businesses can go to extreme lengths to protect their identity and to ensure that the barrier to entry into the territory remains intact. Not so long ago in Australia, Darrell Lea and Cadburys fought with each other over the colour purple.

If you are a franchisor, then it would be prudent to protect your intellectual property from counterfeiters. This is vital should you be doing well in your business.

Chain stores and franchisors should ideally keep track of the changes in the market and of emergence or disappearance of competitors from the landscape. This information is usually stored in an information bundle that is exchanged by the franchisor when they offer a business opportunity to a franchisee. Most of this information is collected on an ad hoc basis and the responsibility of collecting this information rests on the franchisee once the deal has been done.

The challenge with this approach is that the information about the market and the competition is not accurately maintained within the group. Usually, the purpose of such a document is to put the best foot forward for the deal to be made. Key areas of dispute between franchisor and franchisee in the information exchange may not reflect the true market, or opportunity conditions.

As the needs of the market are addressed by a business and when it is successful, by many other competing businesses, the aspects of service become more and more well-defined.

Once the product or service components become well-defined, competitors' step in to offer niche products and services in the area and rather specialise in and take the market share away. This creates a confusoply – a combination of products and services so difficult that it is nearly impossible to make a like-for-like comparison with another offering.

Businesses start competing on

- **Cost/price:** The connotations are different as price is what the consumer pays and cost it what is posted after taking into account all outgoings.

- **Differentiation:** This includes anything and everything that can make you stand aside: the decor of the place, the uniform of the staff, etc.

- **Perceived differentiation:** KFC, McDonald's, Hungry Jacks,
  Burger King and if you are in Australia, Grill'd, all sell chicken burgers, but Grill'd differentiates itself well by suggesting that they are made with love, Nando's perhaps the range of hot sauces.

Market positioning: Do you want to be seen as a low-end player or a premium provider? You should ask yourself what you want to be and why.

Scope of Business→

Global

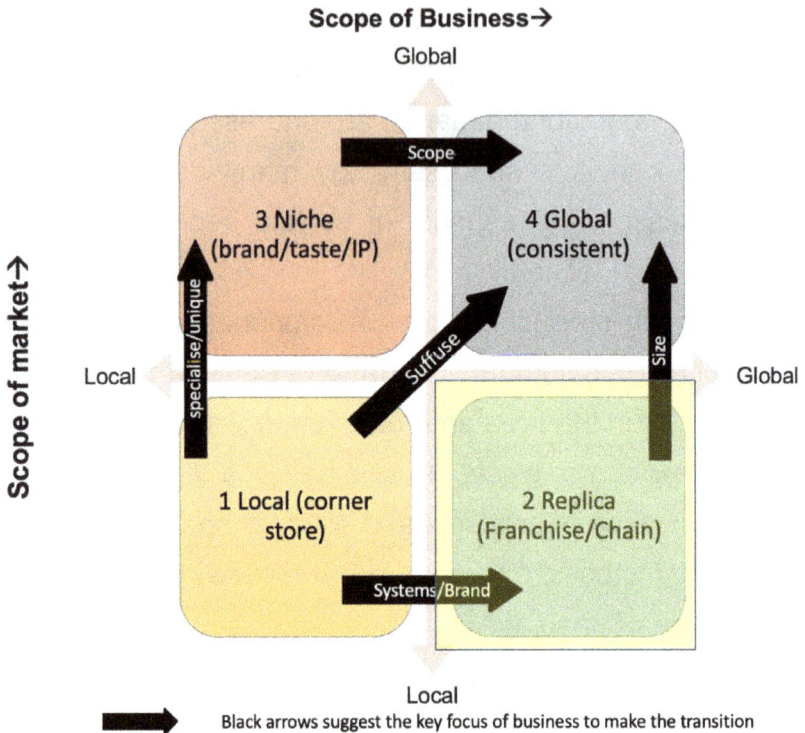

	Scope	
3 Niche (brand/taste/IP)		4 Global (consistent)

Local ← specialise/unique | Suffuse | Size → Global

1 Local (corner store)		2 Replica (Franchise/Chain)
	Systems/Brand	

Local

Black arrows suggest the key focus of business to make the transition

Scope of market→

4. The global store

How do you assess the market for your local store?

Most local businesses start by meeting the unmet needs in a local area, which then becomes competitive if the incumbent business becomes profitable and the market for the products or services becomes well defined (as businesses with similar offerings jump in).

Initially, the business may not have any significant data, so the market is defined based on the assumed target market. This assumed target market can be different from the actual market that provides patronage.

As the business progresses, loyalty and customer data start

becoming available. With competitors joining in, their data also becomes available and although this data may not become a part of your data pool, it can become available from third-party providers including banks and credit card providers and this may add profound value to your business decisions. The data need not necessarily be in the form of filled up rows and columns of sheets, it can also be in the form of inferences drawn after having conversations with a number of visitors and customers.

As you increase the scope of the business to a wider geographic area it is important to observe how it got established in your city. Did it have specific pockets where a particular type of business was stabilised? Or how were the guilds located in the city?

Water has been the catalyst of how a large number of cities got established. A key role was played by irrigation channels, seas, or trade and travel routes.

Market lookalikes play a pivotal role and help grow the business. This relies on the underlying premise of "Birds of a feather flock together." Market lookalikes are two or more areas where the markets are very similar.

If sales are made in an area, there is a greater likelihood of similar customers (customers with similar demographics and psychographics) being in close proximity. The distribution of customers also determines the logistics and growth strategy of a business. If the business is looking at creating territories, the lookalikes will help in creating balanced territories.

Market lookalikes can be identified by running some or all of the following:

- **Market penetration studies** – to locate new opportunities by illustrating the current penetration of customers; finding where the similar ones exist; do they exist in sufficient numbers to install new business.
- **Market gap analysis** – to find market in the gaps, plan media distribution or finding ways to reach them.
- **Spider diagrams** – to identify customer clusters on a map and current business locations that serve these customers. It helps in logistics planning
- **Road travelled diagrams**- Popular roads travelled by customers to ensure the outlet allows easy ingress and egress. It is on the side of the road that links up with customer purchase decisions at the time of travel. As an example, the customers are likely to buy alcohol when they are on course to home from work; if the vehicles travel on the left side of the road it will help to have a shop on the left side of the road allocating for sufficient parking.

Your media coverage or advertising hotspots will also be determined by your market penetration and gap analysis studies. Before you get tempted to advertise in areas where you lack market presence you should ask if your target market exists in that area.

In replicating the success earned at a location it is prudent to pick a market lookalike where demographics and psychographics closely match those of the one found at the successful location.

Think of this as a market fingerprint of an area. For example, in the diagram below A and B are very similar locations while C is quite different. These factors can include anything relevant; for example, customer age, gender, demographics,

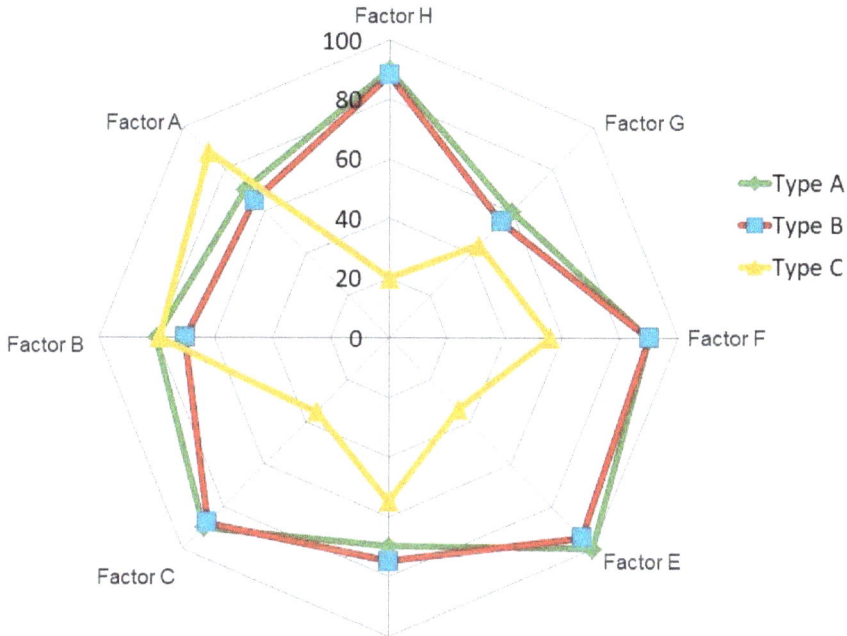

etc. The idea here is that if

we are looking for success, we need to look for similarity in catchments to catchments where success has already been achieved.

When you assess your market on an area you will notice that the size of catchment will change based on the density of population, demographics or how national statistical standards are kept to demark areas (postcodes, regions, states).

The data that you can use to demark may also include information on the business, people, or commercial information.

Sources of this data includes the National Bureau of Statistics, while some other sources of information are registered or unregistered businesses. Market research companies can help you with this information

The important thing to keep in mind here is that though the business may be recording stellar growth, a prudent business owner always validates that the growth is occurring because there is a genuine opportunity rather than being caused by movement of the some business overseas, thus diminishing competition in the pathway to collapse.

When we do not have the real-world data with the requisite depth of information, simulation modelling is used to create demographic or psychographic profile of the residents of a given area. Simulation modelling can use sample data with other data/parameters as proxies.

This is particularly useful when there are gaps in our understanding of the market, demographics, or psychographics. Simulation modelling creates a model to imitate the real world.

An example for daily coffee consumption in Australia using coffee consumption data from a smaller subset of people recording age, demographics and psychographic information. This is iteratively adjusted based on the net consumption in the country to reveal consumption based on demographics and psychographics in each demarked area say SA1[19] level. Indexing or relating the data to a fixed or moving benchmark helps in assessing how a business may be performing *vis à vis* the competition or the market. We live in a dynamic world and analysing our business in comparison to the market helps identify the best- or worst-performing areas in the market territory or catchment.

The results are picked relative to the best or worst in the market:

- To market average
- Normalised to area
- Normalised to population
- Normalised to events or phenomena

These are then visualised as Choropleth maps or heat maps. A dataset in any given area is at index under- or over-indexed to the reference. The over- or under-indexed value shows more or less of the parameter we are measuring. For example, if we are indexing to average population density, or population divided by area, then the areas that are over-indexed will have higher population density and the ones that are under-indexed will have low population density. Consumption of product in this case is measured in per capita terms.

Indexation to the market average helps is suggesting if the business is improving or diminishing in comparison with others.

For example, if you have multiple stores and you want to find out how well a business is running, instead of comparing pure

---

[19] Details available from the Australian Bureau of Statistics

revenue it will help to index based on the number of customers, profit per customer, revenue per customer, cash flow per customer, etc.

It is easier to monitor the indexed values over time, as it gives a true indication of how value is being created and appropriated. It also helps to clarify whether the business is shifting in the positive direction or the market is moving up or down.

CHAPTER 3

Your customers are the reason you are in business

Targeting your customers

If the mountain will not come to Muhammad, then Muhammad must go to the mountain
-Francis Bacon.

Market
Exists

Customers
Don't exist

1 Drive Throughs Transitional	**2** Centralised Competitive
4 Barren/ Opportunity	**3** Targeting/ Gap

Customers
Exist

Market
Doesn't exist

Market and customer collision matrix for an area

For a business to be successful, either the customers should come to the business or the business should go to the customers. This topic examines the interplay of customers and the market at a location. The diagram below shows the different ways in which the customers and the market can coexist.

Horizontal axis represents customer in relative increasing number which are negligible on the extreme left (or don't exist) moving to the right customers exist in increasing numbers.

Vertical axis represents market size which at the bottom represents negligible (or don't exist) moving to the top increasing to large numbers.

As businesses and customers need to come together for a transaction to take place, an ideal place would be where customers and markets coexist in large numbers. That said let us look at complete set of scenarios.

1. Transitional Customers

The market exists and the customers don't exist; this is akin to petrol stations on a long drive, midway restaurants and tourist locations. The traffic or customers in such locations is brought by driving them through. Perhaps I'm taking a very purist point of view when I say that all the customers in an area or tourists are just passing through. The customers are not co-located with the markets; they are simply passing through or visiting briefly from other parts of the planet.

Over time, these hubs continue to bring customers from all around and gradually the local population builds (settles) into the area, who may, in turn, become the consumers of products and services, although not necessarily in a significant proportion.

A very good example here would be Disneyland, or the Gold Coast in Australia, which offers Movie World, Dreamworld, Wet and Wild World and similar services to the world and people tend to travel to that area from all over to enjoy activities

Transportation network holds the key to business opportunity with regard to how traffic is created and moves. As a business, you need to understand and measure this flow and take advantage of the opportunity it brings. It is also important to note how the transport network it gets established and how people move from work to home and vice versa. In order to identify clusters where people are living or working, or areas where they're passing through, helps leverage the traffic flow for business.

If you are delivering products such as groceries to a physical location, then you need to be mindful of who pays the cost of delivery (or is responsible for pick up).

Though new models are emerging rapidly, understanding them will improve the bottom line. If you are exploring online orders and physical delivery, you must note that Amazon is currently trialling a system that will deliver within 30 minutes of placing the order, even in remote locations, by using drones. The best way you can beat that is by differentiating your products or services enough to make them desirable and making sure your secret sauce is not replicable.

Rail network, road network, air network, sea network and foot travel bring opportunities. The information on how the customers are coming when do they come and what the motivations to buy are help leverage them.

As most cities were established around water and different cities have got different shapes based on terrain and topography, Venice looks like fishbones, Delhi has a radial arrangement and New York and Manhattan are quadrangles. You can also have a parallel system, of roads, a loop system of roads, serpent, or tree-shaped networks. Transportation networks are not only the lifelines of an economy; they are lifelines for any given business and you should be leveraging them to the maximum for your benefit.

Foot traffic is one of the less analysed, but very well understood key criteria for impulsive buying that happens in retail. Don't get me wrong – the size of the bill does not have to be small. Impulsive purchases can happen whether the cost of products runs in tens or hundreds of thousands of dollars. People who hang out to cause foot traffic on such streets do attract a higher rent. It is just that impulsive buying as a behaviour means that somebody is passing by, there are goods or items available on the shelf and the customer is enticed to acquire them.

The focus is more on immediate gratification and thus the higher the number of "right" people, the greater the visibility and the larger is the likely number of buyers. An example in this case would be ice cream shops. Most kids, when they see an ice cream shop, they want to get one. For similar reasons, most McDonald's are located in areas of high foot traffic or high pass-through regular traffic area, with golden arches increasing their visibility from miles away.

If you are looking for clues as to how you can measure foot traffic in a business, look for Google.

Google records the MAC addresses of the mobile phones and computers in an area and it keeps track of the number of units that are moving within an area at any given point in time and that in turn results in figures for traffic volume. Although the absolute figures are not given, the relative figures are available. If you run a Google search on any business, you may be able to find foot traffic information relatively easily.

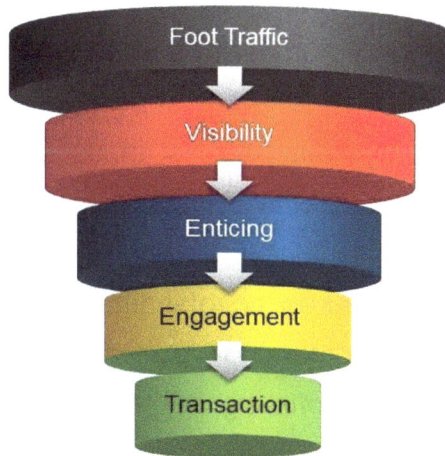

As an analogy, street buskers use a similar strategy. To leverage the foot traffic in an area they usually go and park themselves in the midst of reasonable foot traffic. They entice people to come close to them. They increase their visibility and engage with the customer to keep them participate and keep the engagement going. The show must then begin in order to keep the engagement, or the gathering walks off.

To get more people through the business, greater visibility to the "right" customer helps. Followed by greater engagement to entice them and that's when you will have greater probability of high-volume, high-value transactions occurring.

2. Centralised and competitive market

In this case, a competitive environment exists, as our customers and the markets are trying to reach out to each other with the view to transact at the same time, like in a central business district.

Businesses offer customers similar or identical products or services and customers seeking similar products then compare them on a number of parameters, including service levels and price.

Competition brings out the best in us and business alike. Understanding competitive intensity is vital for business success. High competitive intensity is good when a business is co-located and makes the total attraction of an area higher, thereby pulling customers from a greater distance away. Hubs or market clusters[20] offering a specific niche start forming. Shopping Towns is one such example, where a lot of shops, doing similar business and are at times competing, are co-located.

The current practice in the market is to rank businesses based on revenue and profits. This practice often extends to making

---

[20] Clusters and the New Economics of Competition, by Michael E. Porter *HBR*, November-December 1998

investment or exit decisions. It is prudent to add another dimension of potential based on the market it serves. This will require an understanding of the location of the business and its immediate catchment. The business may continue to perform in ideal situations. If they are not performing well in high-potential areas, they can be improved by redesign.

Businesses in low-potential and low-income categories need an exit from the market. For the business that demonstrates low potential but is demonstrating high income, though it needs to be studied in depth, a better outcome is achieved if it is harvested to   the maximum.

The following figure explains the approach that can be taken in a market where revenue trends are known for a business and market potential can be measured (using demographics, consumption pattenerns and modelling the data). The key advantage in this approach is that it is easier to map the market potential and revenue growth. We do not compare the business with other business however map it against the opportunity itself. This insular approach to business with respect to market potential focusses on   revenue maximisation.

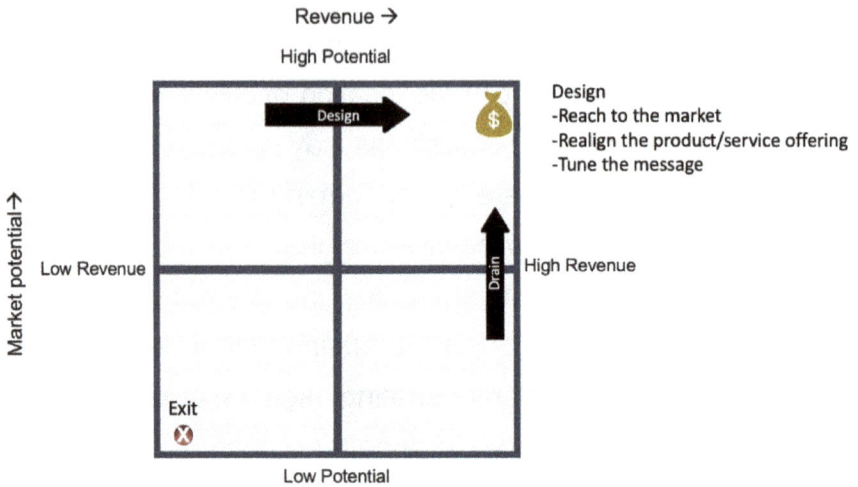

Revenue →

High Potential

Design
- Reach to the market
- Realign the product/service offering
- Tune the message

Market potential →

Low Revenue | High Revenue

Design

Drain

Exit

Low Potential

3. Markets don't exist, but the customers do exist.

The challenge here may be that the number of customers is small or sporadic in terms of their preferences, which prevents a physical outlet from being sustainable. The opportunity here is ripe for either a delivery service to the particular group of customers, or for an online service.

Do understand what scenarios apply in case of your business. It helps businesses to be constantly tune in to the market and by using loyalty cards, Twitter, Facebook, blogs and social media accounts to identify where the customers are and what they're talking about.

The Dabba system[21] in Mumbai is a classic study in this regard, as the customers wanted to have home-cooked meals, which made the existence of outlets untenable. However, turning that into a service by connecting each person to their own home-cooked food has created a unique

---

[21] Mumbai's Models of Service Excellence, by Stefan Thomke. *HBR*, November 2012

business and opportunity for many involved in the business.

> The Dabbawala service is legendary for its reliability. Since it was founded in 1890, it has endured famines, wars, monsoons, Hindu-Muslim riots and a series of terrorist attacks. It has attracted worldwide attention and visits by Prince Charles, Richard Branson and employees of Federal Express, a company renowned for its own mastery of logistics.

4. Neither the customer nor the market exists.

There are few possibilities that exist in such a scenario:

- The area is unlikely to have any opportunity as it may be barren (from an opportunity perspective)
- The opportunity may exist in such an area, but it has not yet been identified.

Areas that are barren or completely devoid of any business opportunity can be turned creatively into a new opportunity area.

This requires sunk cost in the areas where opportunity and customers are non-existent, a completely new venture creation from scratch and then bootstrapping the venture as it starts picking up. As the business picks up in the area, the areas in the immediate vicinity become more valuable. The business needs to keep the future options in mind to leverage the upside.

Matching customers and the opportunity have the classic example of the establishment of Disneyland. It was one simple idea, but a very compelling one, that a place that people from all over the world come to enjoy as a happy place. It required a lot of initial capital investment to bring the idea to fruition. Now kids all over the world know about Disneyland.

In the Greater Springfield area in Australia, Mha Sina Thamby created a massive housing complex. There were no customers to start with – there was no business. It was just barren land, but by bringing and seeding the opportunity, which of course required a huge amount of initial investment, the opportunity was created.

As a business owner, reflecting on the location of your business and its interplay with the market is helpful. It is also helpful when you are making store opening and closing decisions, where understanding the potential in conjunction with the current outcome can set you up well for the long-term game.

Communicating with your customers and prospects

You go to the deep jungle to find a lion. How do you know it's a lion and not a monkey? Because someone told you, or you read it in a book. In much simpler terms, you asked someone about a lion, or someone told you about it.

A similar analogy applies to business. When you are communicating with your market, you should *ask* and *tell*: Ask to understand the expectations and tell to let your market know that how well your offering or your customer experience is aligned to their expectations.

Johari Window

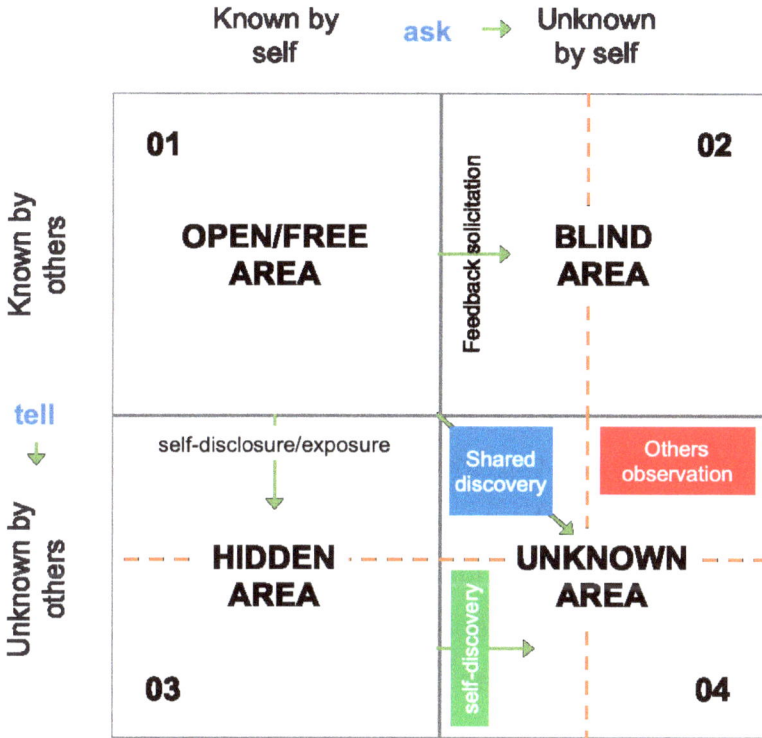

Combining the process of asking and telling will help you create the desired impact. This is better explained by the Johari window[22] (see above), which is an exercise in increasing awareness.

To give the right message to the right market at the right time, we need to ensure the message is relevant and tailored to the

---

[22] Joseph Luft (1916–2014) and Harrington Ingham (1916–1995)

audience. If you recall the first chapter, it is an alignment of the message going out to the market and the perception the market has about the message.

In order to "tell", or share the information, about your business you can reach out to your customers via

- Advertising
- Feedback
- Response to questionnaires.

You can ask your customers about their expectations via

- Market research
- Self-disclosure on online forms
- Social media.

Aligning the offering with the market consumption now and in the future yields the best impact. (Does that mean you need to have a lens into future? Yes Absolutely!) Though businesses measure expectation based on what the customer needs or expresses, it can be misleading. If Henry Ford had asked his customers what they wanted, they would have asked for faster horses. If you uncover what customer wants and what it means for business, your job will be much easier. Hence, asking the customer can be misleading. Understanding your customers' expectations and where your offering fits is where the value lies.

McDonald's follows the Ask-Tell principle to improve the accuracy of drive-throughs.

At Singapore airport, you can provide feedback on toilet cleanliness by way of smileys. It's very easy to engage and understand the consumers and easy to implement. The backend processes help make decisions on frequency and level of cleaning needed.

Telling your customers with signage

These are some very simple ideas to ensure your signage stays meaningful and helps you to attract your customers.

1. **Size**: A large signage allows the customers to see it from a greater distance away. For example, you can see McDonald's golden arches from kilometres away driving at 100 km/hr.

2. **Font**

- **Font Size:** The larger the font size the easier it is to see. However, you need to make sure it is easy to read.

- **Font type:** Very ornate designs, though they may appear impressive, are hard to read and difficult to understand, especially in a scenario where traffic is moving really fast.

- **Font spacing:** If the letters are too close together then it becomes very difficult to tell one from the other and hence readability declines.

3. **Contrast:** The contrast between the background and foreground will help with the readability.

4. **Colour:** It sets the mood and has the ability to suggest invitation (cooler colours like greens). Warmer colours can be used to reflect a soothing feeling. The context in which colours are used can reflect a different feel

for the business.

5. **Numbers:** If you are using street numbers and your business has many lookalikes in the area, you should ensure that the number is displayed prominently. It may not impact walk-ins, but if your prospects and customers are coming from a further distance away, not knowing the number may lead to buying friction and potential switching if there are similar shops in the area.

6. **Location:** Is it at the street intersection, at the crossroad? Inside the curve, or outside the curve? The location plays an important role in the visibility of signage.

7. **Gaming the system:** Purpose is to trick customers without misleading them. The brilliance of this idea is seen in the example of Chemist Warehouse banner (for picture please see Chapter 2) which reads" Is this? Australia's Cheapest Chemist?" gives an impression that it may be the cheapest store.

8. **Zoning regulations:** These may prevent lit-up signs or animated signs, or there may be a limit on the size of signage you can use. Some heritage buildings may have additional constraints.

9. **Property owner regulations:** Multi-tenant properties, or in the case of mixed usage or for any other reasons, owners may constrain the type and size of the signage used. In many cases, owners may like to standardise the signage and charge a fee and control the process.

10. A heritage area may have its restrictions and constraints, for example on the visibility of façades. Please check with your council regarding this.

11. **Multitenant confusion:** If offering the same service to multiple tenants (to a doctor, for example) standardisation (of name plate) is essential.

12. **Trees:** Trees can block the view to the shopfront, while giving refuge to an array of birds, whose droppings may be unsightly. It may be an area where hawkers may be active, so signboards that detract may be placed. it's important to ensure that you do not encounter any of these negative issues.

13. **Creating a replicable ambience:** McDonald's - arches, driveways, speaker systems, uniformed staff, play areas of similar colour and even standardised questions such as, "You want fries with that?" or, "You want to upsize?"

Relationship with customers:
Loyalty vs promiscuity

For any given business there is a greater likelihood of getting customers from close proximity to the store. The likelihood decreases as we go further from the store. The size of the proximity varies from business to business.

For example, all being equal, you are more likely to buy groceries from a shop next door than the one that is miles away, provided that prices, availability and other elements are comparable.

Secondly, the preference to travel a distance varies from product to product, all other things being equal. For example, you are likely to be prepared to travel a shorter distance to buy a cup of coffee than to buy a piece of furniture. This is related to the materiality of the transaction and the impulse required for purchase.

Research done by a charity organisation indicated that materiality plays a significant part in distance travelled, with the exception of tourism (or in instances where discretion is involved). A similar scenario applies when shopping: Spending increases only then people are prepared to travel greater distances.

The other interesting observation on my projects was that the distance travelled also depends on the time it takes to get to the destination. The price the driver has to pay to deal with congestion also impacts on the purchase decision.

Type of location determines where a business gets its customers from. Low value and a large number of transactions represent impulsive purchases. The impact of impulse will vary based on the disposable income of people in that area. It is essential that one measures the number of passers-by who are impulse buyers and fall into the target market category.

We cannot discount the agglomeration effect here when a person who may be flying in from interstate or another continent to visit a local destination engages in impulsive purchasing.

These impulsive transactions usually come in a bundle, or in an *impulsive disposable bundle* that exhibits its trait multiple times within a day, or in the duration of a visit, according to what any given visitor has budgeted.

Getting a good handle on this topic helps in levelling up a business. You may have seen that many hotels or resorts are built far away from major habitation areas to keep the real estate costs lower and also to keep the guests in to take advantage of their discretionary budget. The distance they may be required to travel for other purchases is huge. The same effect can be observed at a smaller level, with relatively very high in-room minibar prices where the distance required to travel to get a substitute product is high that said the impulse for instantaneous gratification is also high.

However, you will observe that the restaurants and hotels that are within the vicinity of other shops tend to keep their prices marginally higher and run pricing models so that maximum value flows to them.

Customer loyalty and life time business value

Your relationship with your customers is very similar to your close relationships akin to a spouse or partner. You are looking for a two-way commitment which is beneficial to both.

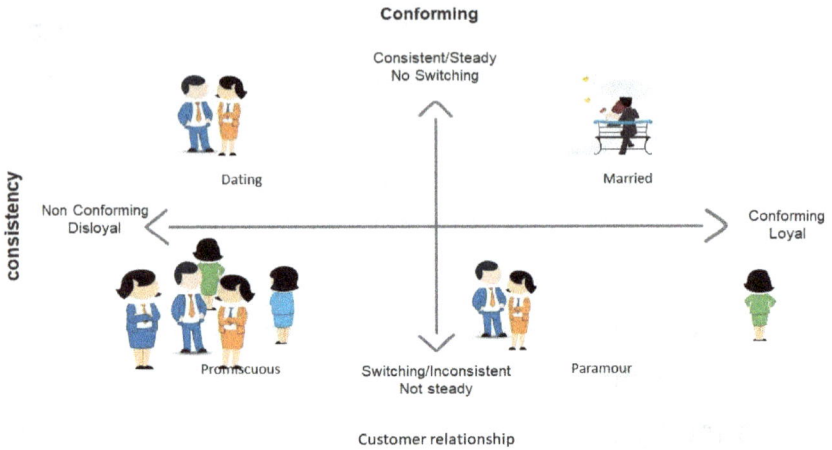

Customer relationship

Extending this analogy to business we can see the relationship a business has with the customer it can fall in four different types:

The model above portrays how customers like or prefer to shop at different shops. In the diagram, the horizontal axis represents conformity (moving from least conformal on the left to most conformal on the right) and the vertical axis consistency (moving from least consistency at the bottom increasing in consistency to the top). Think of it as if it is a tap: That tap can have water coming out at a very ambient temperature it is in conformity. The tap can have water flowing in a steady stream of flow, which is consistency.

If the temperature stays ambient all the time, the flow will be steady, the outcome will be pleasant all the time. Like a happy marriage, everything is predictable. In a shopping scenario, customer lifetime value is maximum as it is a perfect relationship between you and your customer.

Second scenario is like a dating relationship: The temperature may vary hot (or cold), but the flow is steady. The customers category might still love to buy from the shop when the need arises, but a steady pattern has not yet emerged. It's like when trying to eat out Chinese food, you may prefer to go the same restaurant (but you may not prefer to eat Chinese food all the time).

The third scenario is analogous to a promiscuous relationship. There is no warmth and the flow changes erratically. People are shopping around then experimenting; they're looking for a quick bargain and sometimes they're not sure what they want. They go window shopping, check things out and ask for prices. Then may end up buying the stuff online.

The fourth scenario is similar to a paramour relationship: The temperature is ambient, but the flow is not steady. Customers love the brand or the shop, but they may want more. In a consumption paradigm they may move between brands for the same purpose. Sometimes the paramour gets upgraded to a partner. An example here is users moving from a Ford car to a Lexus to a Ferrari. The relationship with brand changes with change in wealth and disposable income so the same person may shift preferences or may end up consuming multiple products for the same desired outcome (more bells and whistles).

Based on the research by A C Karunaratna at the University of Ruhuna[23], the key factors that can cause customers to switch are

- inferior quality;
- stock unavailability;

---

[23] Propensity to customer switching: a review on apparel stores, by A C. Karunaratna. *European Journal of Business and Economics* (2015). 10. 10.12955/ejbe. v10i2.695

- service failure;
- stressful atmosphere;
- High prices.

CHAPTER 4

Key focus of any business hould be of Creating Monopoly

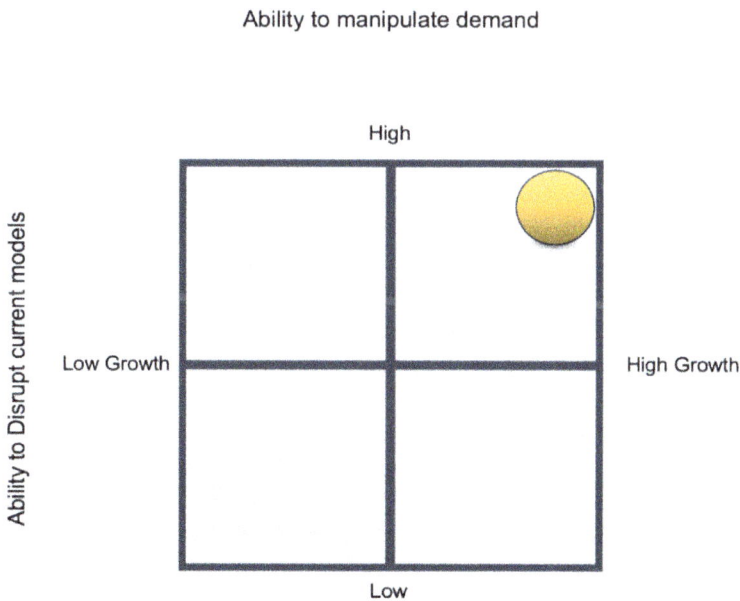

Ability to manipulate demand

High

Low Growth | High Growth

Low

Ability to Disrupt current models

Once established as a business, your sole purpose should be to turn   it into a monopoly. Your business can be a monopoly in your street, suburb, country or worldwide (in the category and market you serve).

As a monopoly, you will challenge the existing business models that prevail and control and manipulate the demand. This is be done by appealing to their emotions rather than the features. "Oh, what a feeling" is the advertisement that Toyota has been using. The evident emotional appeal is very explicit. Businesses deploy the following seven-step process to create an absolute monopoly:

1. Create demand.
2. Raise barriers for competition.
3. Create confusion in the market about your strategy.
4. Customer lock-in.
5. Restrict supply to increase category demand.
6. Appear to be competing with self.
7. Breaking the existing monopoly/barriers.

Some online examples in this include

- **Amazon** looks at the products that are doing exceptionally well in its stores and in many cases comes up with better and more economical products to service the same market.

- **Apple** leverages the ideas and features that are either submitted by the developers on its marketplace or from other open-source products, or even at times, competitors' products.

- **Uber** has destroyed the competition by introducing a product that was pretty good for the market. It lowered the barriers for cab drivers, made the services available at a lower cost and made purchase frictionless (customers can walk away). As a result, the existing cabs have become almost extinct in many parts of the world. As the cabs cease to exist at the required levels that the market needs and the dependence on Uber grows, it is able to charge surge pricing.

- **Airbnb** used rapid growth and network effect to reach out to the market and create an absolute monopoly.

- **Facebook** created a new category of *likes* and now people are paying money to get likes on their social media profile. It adds to their prestige and brand recognition without necessarily adding to bottom line revenue.

- **Pablo Escobar** freely supplied drugs in the United States and got people addicted so that they then bought them at high prices. He used drugs and leveraged this market position to create a monopoly.

Last example has negative connotations, however the approach taken is to get people used to a product or service in a niche or a location, to make them highly dependent and then charge exceptionally for the offering. Though such practices are illegal, many modern-day businesses are using elements of the same tactics (or its variants), albeit legally.

1: Creating Demand

Creating demand is a key step towards creating a monopoly. How do businesses create demand? The following eight business ideas may suggest just a few of the ways:

1. **Create artificial scarcity (or leverage on scarcity)** create an environment where people may have a fear of missing out on the offer or the price, or some aspect of the offering that makes them feel they may be worse off if they do not act in time. Apple benefited very well from the hype when the news channels showed long queues in front Apple stores, suggesting limited stock availability.

2. **Get users to create their own content and contribute:** The consumer becomes the part of the business and has skin in the game. Many businesses get customers or their kids to colour a picture and post it on their wall. Kids love it they want to take their whole family to shop where their painting is placed on the wall. As a collateral, they get repeat business and get to know the whole family. Family restaurants are quite famous for that. In a lot of physical stores as well as online stores, the members who sign up get a discount, free delivery or the like. The reciprocal advantage is that once a user signs up to the loyalty scheme, feedbacks and any posted pictures on social media act as endorsements and help in attracting other customers.

3. **Exclusivity:** I am sure you have come across the scenario where designers produce only a limited number of designs or pieces of handbags, clothes or shoes and are exclusive[24] to a territory, market or exclusive by being limited in supply. There is a race among the customers to get in first to get their hands on their preferred item. Many leading fashion brands destroy their unsold items to maintain exclusivity, instead of discounting them. Early-release or new-season products follow the same pattern. In addition, they exploit the higher willingness to pay early on to appropriate greater returns.

4. **Impact on life:** Better or cheaper or faster? Amazon Stores now allow you to walk in and out of their new stores without using designated checkouts. Reducing the friction allows customers to easily walk through and moreover, any combination of better, cheaper and faster allows differentiation. If you want it easy, think lazy.

5. **Brand association:** Using a Rockstar as a role model, users create a natural attraction from many to be like their idols.

6. **Newness paradigm:** Some customers want to stay ahead of the game; they are early adopters, or risk-

---

[24] Exclusivity is another secret to the success of the brand. Louis Vuitton has always tried to counter mass production with short-term limited-edition series. This means that not everyone will own the same bags and means that those who do get their hands on a limited-edition bag, get fantastic exclusivity. When products come out in small numbers, a buzz is created instantly, and people crave the latest style of bag. Because of this scarcity, waiting lists become longer and longer and the products even more desirable. Source: Catawiki.com

takers. Seth Godin calls them sneezers[25] These are also discussed as early adopters in the book *Crossing the Chasm*[26]. People try and keep up with various versions of iPhone just to look cool and in tune with the market. For many of these types, not upgrading means not changing with the times.

7. **Emotive appeal:** "Oh, what a feeling, Toyota!" It is no longer about the product but what it brings. Nike is tapping into the emotion of "greatness. Once the user's mind is associated with the keyword that the business is using, any occurrence of that word reminds them of the brand or product. If I said, "Don't think about the pink elephant," I wonder what you would then think about. To get deep in the concept, you may want to have a look at *Purple Cow* by Seth Godin.[27]

8. **Creating commitment:** Remember the competitions where one describes in X words or less and you get a reward. Well, you do get a reward in exchange for convincing yourself why should you buy/use/travel/express an interest in something offered. It is going to stay with you for the rest of your life, as you have just managed to convince yourself. It is a very well discussed topic by Cialdini.[28] As a business, this requires initial cost outlay but is a good brand-building strategy

---

[25] *Unleashing the Idea Virus*, by Seth Godin, 2000, Seth Godin

[26] *Crossing the Chasm*, by Geoffrey A. Moore, 2009, Harper Collins

[27] *Purple Cow*, by Seth Godin, 2005

[28] *Influence*, by Robert B. Cialdini, 1988

2: Raising barriers for competition

Incumbent players create a barrier to entry or prevent other businesses from encroaching on the lucrative market or its customers.

There are many different mechanisms by which many businesses achieve it. A set of nine of these methods is listed below:

1. **Control the cost of the supply chain and do better than your competition:**

- Collaborating with other similar businesses to participate in the procurement of goods, delivery, despatch of products, or any other aspect of your supply chain that allows synergies. You supply to your competition to give them a slight cost advantage although you lower your total cost of ownership. For example, a New Zealand hotel chain invested in infrastructure to wash and fold sheets at a significantly lower price for their internal purposes. To break even they needed twice the volume of work. They reached out to their competition and offered them a lower price than they were already paying and got them to switch. At the same time, they continued to invest in similar infrastructure. Now they have monopoly in the laundry business in their town. They have managed to reduce their cost while adding a new competitive edge to their value chain.

- Segment the supply chain performance based on customer, markets, industries and products and redesign it if needed. Each of the segments requires a varying degree of timeliness, risk, complexity, volume and profitability. Identification of segments helps in eliminating a segment of customers or the market that is not profitable.

- Measure every component of the business and then compare it with industry benchmarks. It will help identifying areas that need operational improvements. As a simple example, it is estimated that 28% of supply chain costs are incurred in the last mile of the business and getting it wrong can impact the bottom line, or erode the profit completely.

2. **Vertical integration** reduces transaction costs. An extreme example here is that of Starbucks, which has coffee bean farms, coffee bean roasting plants, warehouses and distribution plants and the well-known retail outlets. It may not always be possible to have a fully vertically integrated business but is always a good strategy when feasible. You control the game end to end and manage the quality, the service, the intellectual property, the processes, the workflow – the lot. The flipside is cost, but some businesses, such as rice merchants in India, have overcome that by providing initial loans to farmers and a commitment to buy at an agreed price should their produce be of a certain quality. It gives committed business to

farmers with initial money to play with, at the same time it gives an indication of committed supply volume at a cost where the merchants hedge their bets in the national or international markets with a huge commercial upside.

3. **Bringing regulation in your favour:** With regulatory forces supporting your endeavour puts your business in a powerful position. The business may control assets and infrastructure, which are hard to replace. The business runs like a true monopoly. Examples include banks, post offices infrastructure that are controlled by government in many countries.

4. **Enjoying subsidies:** Car companies in Australia, including Holden, enjoyed excellent subsidies from the government. Holden had the advantage of subsidy. However, if we combine the entire car industry in Australia, every fifth Australian household would have got a free car however the benefits reaped by car companies.

5. **Tariffs:** Tariffs are introduced on products coming from overseas. Though tariffs do not protect in the long run, they do give you short- run immunity from global market forces. If you are based in Australia, you may not be able to compete with the cost of labour coming from the third world, as the individual workers may originate from a place offering lower human development index, which comes at a lower cost. *As a country, GDP depends on natural resources, entrepreneurship, literacy and physical and human*

capital. Developed economies should record a higher GDP growth due to intellectual capital and entrepreneurship growing at an accelerated pace; it is not always the case and hence protectionism is needed to selectively safeguard the wealth of the country.

6. **Intellectual property protection:** Intellectual property or patent can be protected and is essential and prevalent in IT and drug companies. Protection needs registration that introduces the risk of copying. If you have a secret sauce it is a good idea to keep it secret, if you try and patent it, the chances that others might be able to copy re-produce it are high. The Coca-Cola recipe, for example, is still a closely guarded secret. Large firms with a bigger war chest use IP to thwart competition. It is a known practice to drag competition in legal warfare to compel them to spend their marketing budgets in legal costs

7. **Real estate or other key physical assets:** Assets control what happens in and around them. As the asset's value appreciates the businesses all around benefits. If you are looking at installing a greenfield outlet you're better off buying the whole chunk of real estate around it, or if you're establishing a restaurant in the middle of a highway it's a good idea to have control of the purchase of the assets and not just the rentals. As the area develops, the total attraction of the place will increase and will start a virtuous cycle. By controlling key assets in the area, you will gain in

the long run when assets appreciated in value relative to the market.

8. **Speed of execution:** This model prevails in the technology and software industries. Particularly when the business is simple, rapidly growing and tempting competition to copy the strategy. It is very easy to replicate the success of an incumbent's business. Creating a complex web of relationships and elements that are very hard to replicate can be difficult to implement if a business model is very simple. Constantly produce minor improvements and come up with new features and offerings at a rapid rate to outsmart the competition.

9. **Making it easy to buy:** This is perhaps the simplest to understand, but complex to implement. This entails reducing or removing all the friction to complete the transaction. If a continuous supply of products or services is required, then the delivery to customers should be on autopilot (delivery of fruit and vegetable basket – twice a week to customer's doorstep). You should ideally map your customers' journey from initial engagement to purchase. If ongoing service or assistance is needed, then you need to map the entire lifecycle subsequently, look at each touchpoint and simplify the engagement process. The backend processes need to be reviewed simultaneously to provide positive and seamless experience or outcome for your customer. Here is a very simplified example to depict a customer journey for a software purchase

decision. Customers will prefer to buy from you than your competition even at a marginally higher price provided the purchase process easier for them

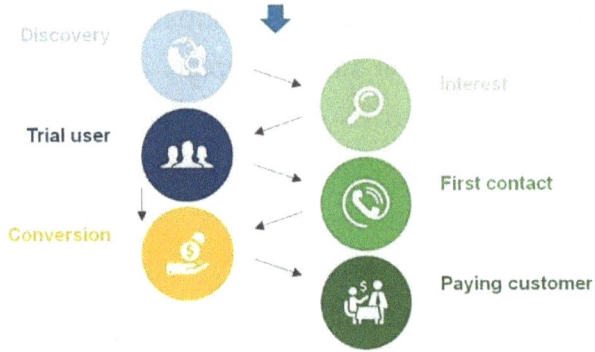

3. Creating confusion in the market about your strategy

If you're a truly monopolistic business, you should try and mislead the market, as it helps the market to miscalculate your market share and your moves.

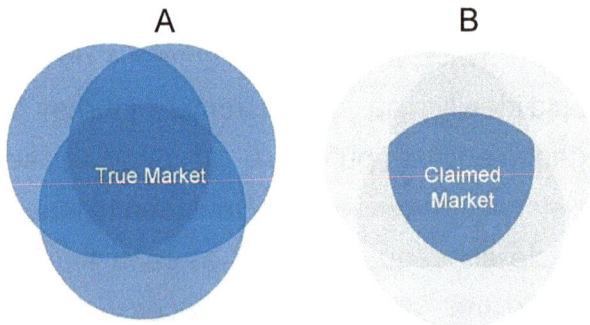

Monopolistic companies pretend to compete in fewer domains than they are actually participating in and competitive firms focus on unique selling proposition. Tendency to shift the market perception is high in successful firms. If you look at the

diagram, it shows that conglomerate monopolistic business pretends to play in space "B" and not in "A" claiming a smaller market than they actually play in.

Though focussed on start-up Peter Thiel's book "Zero to One" is recommended. If you look at companies like Google, they created an enormous amount of confusion about whether it's a search engine, whether it's an advertising engine, or whether it's a firm selling in information technology products. Now their Alphabet business does the same.

4: Customer lock in

Online customer lock in: Consider a scenario of customer rating. For example, eBay allows customers to be given a star rating and Google allows rating to be given to a business. Businesses in any location can be given stars and it's very difficult for people to keep changing their Business because then they have to run the whole process of gaining those stars. Likewise, there are a lot of rating sites out there that help businesses get good ratings and climb up in the rank. Changing the rating provider means you restart your ranking profile from a clean slate and changing your business means losing the ranking and starting over again. Rating systems act as asset. However, they stay in the public domain offering visibility. There is inherent inability in the process to remove your rating assets (belongings). Some professionals and businesses have found ways to prevent their information to be listed anywhere, which helps them tell the stories they like and allows them to keep changing their stories. However, for

20year old's, if they don't see information online, the existence may not be important enough for their world to take note of. Play well on the social rating mechanisms, it is a poor strategy to have fake ratings, followers or likes, others will be able to smell them a mile away and you will end up chasing fake customers for business, losing the real ones to your competition.

Product component driven lock in: The disposable pod-based coffee machine is another cool example. One may buy a cheap coffee machine; however, compatible pods will be needed which may be expensive. Hence customer can be locked in with a cheap (or free) machine and expensive pods. The same applies to printers that that can be bought at a cheap price, but when you go to buy ink cartridges, they are super expensive. You create a lock-in by offering one component of your product or service cheaper and making the other component more expensive. A similar example in the products industry is the QWERTY keyboard. The QWERTY keyboard came into existence because the keys were getting jammed owing to the speed at which people could type and product designers had to find a way to slow down the process. They were able to slow down the process by messing it up and the result was the QWERTY keyboard. However, it became a standard that we haven't changed since.

Convenience based lock in: Free to sign up; provide your credit card; first delivery completely free; cancel anytime; by devising deals like this the purpose of your business is to sell convenience and quality and ensure they stay as an ongoing customer. Though the first offer stays free, the statistics for cancellation are not very high in this type of promotion.

Loyalty based lock in: Your business can sell coffee mugs for $5 and every time customers come for a refill, they are discounted by 20%. And so, you as long as you have the coffee cup branded with your own brand, you are likely to get their business over competing businesses. Getting your brand promoted on someone's desk – priceless! The process entices customers to shop regularly, so they become loyal customers without knowing. If they switch, they lose the benefit.

If your loyal customers shift to another business, they suddenly lose the advantage that they were getting. The new business (or business chain) that your customers have switched to will not only have to compete in terms of products and features, but also on the benefits the loyalty program that was already available to customer.

Information and skill-based lock in: You can create **skills** in learning about product and services. For example, in the case of Bunnings in Australia, they run very successful training programs. When we had Masters competing with them in Australia, Masters were focussing on products. At Bunnings, the training program augmented with skilled trades that consulted with customers who brought prospects and customers again and again to Bunnings to create skills-driven lock-in. As a result, Bunnings runs as a large consulting house that sells products, whilst Masters was an outlet selling products.

Standardisation based lock in: When you go to chain stores, the layout is pretty identical. So, no matter which branch you are shopping in, it looks pretty much similar. Likewise, many other businesses have an identical network of placement within the shop floor, which creates a familiarity. Standardisation is predominant in McDonald's. The look and feel of every McDonald's store (though they have their own differentiation), is quite similar. The play area is very similar among different stores. As long as the standardisation is maintained, people feel connected with the brand and show familiarity with the product or service being provided.

The exit fees based lock in: If you have a shop in the supermarket, or if you're part of a membership group or part of an association, then there may be a small penalty that you have to pay to exit a location or a group and that exit fee prevents people from making low- threshold decisions.

In Australia, Telstra or Optus, among many of the phone companies will offer a new contract before the old one is expired – a deal you cannot easily refuse. Or if you want to change your contract to another provider, you may have to pay exit fees or wait till your iPhone is really old and glitchy. These exit fees can help you keep a hold on your customers ethically.

5. Restrict supply to increase category demand

You can manipulate demand in the market to push prices or demand up in the following ways.

1. **Creating social proof:** If all your friends are on Skype, the chances are you are more likely to be using Skype than any other communication platform. The same applies to heaps of other social media platforms such as Facebook, which builds and feeds off network effects. Likewise, if your friends have a particular type of car or a particular type of TV, or they shop in a particular set of stores, the chances are that you'll also shop in similar types of store. So, if you want to reach a greater degree of control in the market, you need to understand the connectivity between these individuals who hang out together and behave in a similar way.

2. **Helping customers self-select:** This is quite similar to showing the most expensive TV at the front of the store or showing the best product as customers enter the shop and then showing you medium or inferior-quality products. By now your prospective customers have anchored themselves to the best product and possibly the highest price. There is significant work done in this area by Robert Cialdini and his book Influence[29] is highly recommended on the topic. Once your prospective customers have anchored their mind on a more premium-brand or more expensive product or service, or the gold or platinum standard, you then try to show them what other possibilities might exist,

---

[29] *Influence*, by Robert B. Cialdini: Pearson New International Edition

as it's very difficult for them to move away from a higher-value to a lower-value position.

If the higher-value position was shown first and the mind of the prospect is anchored to the value proposition, then everything else seems to be discounted. When you take a flight, you are be paraded through first Business, then Premium Economy to Economy Class, just to be shown what's out there. It shows you what you are missing out on before you put yourself in cattle class, or economy class, seat. It pushes you to score better next time and self-select to put yourself in a category you so much deserve.

3. **Offering reciprocal concessions:** As a club owner, you can offer benefits to other clubs to include discounted or reciprocal membership. You suddenly get to reach a wider market and its customers, so the customers and club both win in this case. Part of being a bigger group brings economies of scale and scope. The chain hotels and motels have this advantage. The advantage of reciprocal concessions sometimes outweighs the disadvantage or inconvenience of odd locations. Hotels being slightly away from prime locations may not feel inconvenient. Customers may not be aware of, or are unlikely to pick, these non-prime locations by default, but as they are getting a huge range of benefits, they are likely to stick to the business that offers reciprocal concessions. My physical trainer has an arrangement with a coffee

shop. He offers coffee vouchers to those who accomplish a milestone. The nearby coffee shop honours these in exchange for a free coffee to patron. The physical trainer gets these vouchers in deeply discounted price in bulk whilst the coffee shop gets extra customers. Everyone wins.

4. **Tiered reward-based consumption uplift:** Your loyal customers get rewards. Two things are bound to happen with loyal customers:

   a. In the terminology of Seth Godin, they become *sneezers* and go and tell others to promote your business (become referrers).

   b. You hammer messages constantly to your loyal customers, relaying their points, entitlements and where they are placed on the ladder. Telling them that they are getting love, care and respect in exchange for their commitment to be your customer.

6. Appearing to be competing with self

As a business, sometimes you have to compete with yourself. The following are a few key reasons:

1. **Constant improvement:** you can constantly bring improved and revised versions of your products. Just like in the software industry, where every year (technology has enabled monthly, weekly, daily and hourly updates) a new version is released. It encourages customers to buy the new product or

service. For example, Tesla as a car company is always coming up with enhancements. That same mindset also attributed to the success of Apple.

The seed of this concept comes from the software industry's dependence on renewal. I will attribute this to Bill Gates. You signed a licence agreement and you were entitled to use the product for a period and then came a new version that you had to buy or pay upgrade costs for. If you didn't upgrade, you missed out. If you upgraded, you paid up. The entire software industry is based around this idea of seeking ongoing payment for ongoing value (and improvements).

2. **Making the competition irrelevant:** It does help when you are competing with yourself that sometimes competition becomes irrelevant, as your visible strategy keeps changing and is differentiated. So, the competition is left with no option but to play catch-up.

3. **Causing lock-in** If you give a customer an unlimited chance to upgrade or change or modify the product, as Costco does (conditions apply), they can return the product if they're not happy or if it's not working. They can return it anytime and now they're locked in, not to the product but to Costco[30]. Because you're not only buying the product, you're buying the insurance as well and you're still paying a smaller amount than you would pay somewhere else.

---

[30] Its exact policy may vary but I have found that the warranty in Australia very generously extends beyond one year.

4. **Dealing with disruption:** The business environment is rapidly changing, and you sometimes have to game it up to ensure that you stand the test of time. You will need to create a business entity, or split the entity, or create similar-looking businesses. You may need to create chain stores around your existing business to thwart competition. Others might be doing exactly the same thing and living up with some degree of cannibalisation of customers.

5. **Raising bar for staff:** Getting your business(es) to compete amongst themselves helps push the staff to higher performance levels and also brings opportunities for them to grow personally and professionally. This also helps expand their mindset to a growth mindset[31], as they are exposed to the wider options that a growing business brings to them.

7.Breaking the existing barriers /monopolies

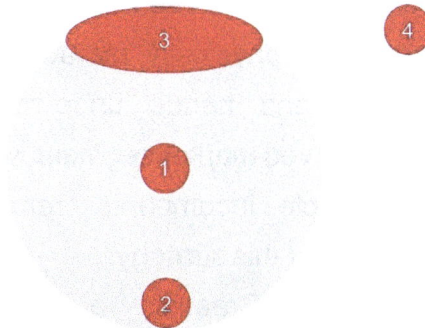

1. Niche
2. Fringe
3. Piggybacking
4. innovating

---

[31] *Mindset* - Updated Edition, Psychology, by Carol Dweck.

There are four likely ways of breaking down barriers to entry laid by existing monopolies. Though it may seem simple, it may be very complex, as the incumbent may be playing on all the four different options by creating, investing, acquiring. or incubating a business. Let's dig deep and understand them better:

1. **Niche:** This can be created based on a set of features, a combination of features or services that is used to target a new segment of customers in the preferred geographic, demographic or psychographic that is open to trying out something new. The creation of the Red Bull drink and the Boost juice chain stores falls into this category that capitalised on the niche to grow the business.

2. **Fringe:** Every business or product has a core set of customers with a high customer lifetime value. Then they have a long tail of customers who are occasional shoppers, switchers, or explorers. These are the customers who are on the fringes; at times these may simply be physically far away from the product or service and hence underserved. Identifying this underserved market segment, where there can be one or multiple incumbents, remains the key to the success of this strategy.

3. **Innovate:** Creating a completely new value proposition is much discussed in the book Blue Ocean Strategy, by Kim and Maubourgne. Creating a new

value proposition makes it difficult for an entrenched incumbent to respond. The incumbent may be complacent because of significant investment and high profits in an existing business. Kodak is the best example here, their business rapidly eroded as it failed to take steps to move into digital technologies. Some recent interesting examples are flat wine bottles: *Garçon Wines flat bottle*; small format convenience stores in proximity which offer a wide range of services (including post shops in Australia), shops that combine multiple services (garden + café).

4. **Piggybacking and association:** Next step to innovation: exposure to large markets where the incumbent partners and benefits significantly from an innovator. This is a win-win for incumbents and new entrants in the market.

CHAPTER 5

Location that results in a Business opportunity

The right location is vital for any bricks-and-mortar business. It can make or break it.

The following 10 key steps help you spot, leverage and maximise the opportunity and dollars that stay hidden in the location of a retail site location.

In a fiercely competitive forum, it is a constant struggle to be heard above the noise. I constantly talk to businesses to consider the question: "Is the message from the business compelling enough for the target market to hear and reach out for products or services?"

We all know that fewer than 25 percent of businesses compete successfully, grow continually and genuinely add true value to the market. This only happens when the message, the market and the mode of engagement are clear and relevant,

A very strategic data-driven investigative process designed to maximise your investments and capitalise on benefits helps. Here are his tips on working with data for success with site selection:

Defining success

Businesses operate under many levels of hierarchy:

- Things that pertain to the store (staff age, number of staff, number of products, how often it is stocked etc.);
- Things pertaining to the site (decisions the business makes, signboards, accessibility, parking, etc.).
- Things pertaining to the trade (demographics, psychographics, population coming in, population going out, tourism, how far the customers are willing to travel, how far the business delivers to customers, etc.)
- Things pertaining to the region (policy changes, major developments etc.). Besides this, there are other geopolitical and national issues that extend to state, or country, or cross-national boundaries.

Without any preconceived bias, the first stage is to brainstorm and list all the potential factors that may positively or detrimentally impact the business in question at a specific location.

Selecting ideal sites

Step 1: Identify the factors for success.

The factors you choose will need to support your end game. You may be looking for expansion or to prioritise your investments. Irrespective of where your preferences lie, the decisions made should consider any upcoming demographic shift. To achieve this, you need data that is accurate, current and of high quality so that the decision will stand the test of time.

You need to understand the following:

- The scope of business both now and in future
- The overserved and underserved markets
- Customer transaction patterns by location, time, product and proximity to store in purchase decisions
- The competitive intensity that may impact the business in question
- Changes in socioeconomic characteristics
- How to tailor the message through the relevant channels.

It is very much like peeling the layers of an onion: You need to keep going as far as you need to go.

Step 2: Understand the trade area.

Retail trade area analysis helps in describing a target market. It is the reach of customers for any given type of business and the resistance to travelling the customers have to overcome to get to the business. For a coffee shop, it can be a few minutes' walk, but it could be a 30-minute drive for a furniture store. Once we understand the catchment area or trade area, we can easily segment the profile of customers in that area and allocate spend against each customer at that location. The accuracy of the model depends on the data used and drive-time data is the most useful.

The trade area is then generated using gravity models that take competitive intensity and attractiveness into account to calculate the probability of customer visits.

Step 3: Isolate and prioritise key factors.

It is imperative that the business understands the relationships between key revenue drivers and trade area demographics, customer profiles, etc. Some of the factors can include bank transition data in a particular category that helps to benchmark consumption.

In the absence of bank data, proxy data depicting the target market, or simulation data, can also be used. Data from multiple sources, including the retailer's own data, with customer information, population, demographics and if needed data from other external providers can be leveraged to identify the positive and negative contributors to the business.

Step 4: Understand the infrastructural issues.

The desirability of a retail location can be based on its centrality and accessibility. It is generally assumed that residents of a place are lookalike, or they share a common demographic and behavioural set of attributes.

The infrastructural or transport factors are looked at based on the type of target market. These factors can include public transport, annual average vehicular traffic, foot traffic and parking.

Step 5: Identify and prioritise profitable areas.

Once the ideal factors are identified, run an algorithm to rank areas where these favourable situations exist.

Irrespective of the population concentrations, the rank ordering suggests that given a set of conditions a business will benefit when located in a higher-rank zone compared to a lower-ranked zone.

Things to keep in mind are competitive store locations (competitive benchmarking), new dwelling approvals, movement of containers, taxation statistics and property sales.

The next step is identifying the best locations within the zones.

Step 6: Benchmark locations.

There is another complex technique to follow is to benchmark the probability of success, adjusting (if needed) based on attractors and repellers for a retail location.

We look at the impact of another contributing asset that enhances (positive or negative) outcomes and we adjust the revenue outcomes accordingly.

It is not a direct deduction that a competitive store will end up negatively impacting the store in question. It has been found that when businesses are co-located, the overall attraction of the area goes up

Step 7: Understand the demographics.

Detailed demographic reports for different areas give a true reflection of what is happening on the ground. An area identified in Step 6 accompanied by a detailed demographic report or any additional and relevant reports helps paint a true picture.

In many cases, different datasets for a region (SA1, SA2[32], postcode, suburb, or a region) based on a criterion are combined to create a location report, prospect store report, franchise report, or any document that franchisors can give to franchise buyers.

Step 8: Market in the gap.

Sometimes looking at "what if" scenarios can help to analyse the impact of new competitors, store consolidation, expansion and cannibalisation.

In the case of franchised stores with multiple locations, specific pockets of opportunity can be looked at by running a gap analysis. This is based on the standard market catchment for the type of business or tailored to the specific needs of the business.

Step 9: Cannibalisation.

It's important to get a balance of distance between outlets. You want to ensure that customers who are on the fringes of

---

[32] Details can be found at: Australian Statistical Geography Standard
https://www.abs.gov.au/geography

an area have an alternative option to shop, particularly if they are in the gaps between the catchments and that fall in lucrative areas.

Too-close proximity of stores, however, may lead to too much cannibalisation and over-investment. This may not be evident in the short term, but as the market saturates it becomes more obvious.

Step 10: Online or digital locations

The same approach applies to the online world. Digital locations are the places that reach the customers in the virtual space; however, the fulfilment may be done in the real world. Important data to provide the right information can include a customer's purchase history, tracking an IP address, monitoring social fingerprints, etc.

Once the digital fingerprint is identified, the rest of the analytical process is very similar to bricks-and-mortar stores.

Using location intelligence to organise and understand complex phenomena and unify it with market analytics and customer analytics helps us to understand trends in customer data, market data and demographics to help form clear, reliable, repeatable views of where emerging opportunity exists in relation to an existing retail network.

Following the above 10 steps will truly give your retail site and your business the edge it needs to be successful in the current age.

Proximity is the key to leveraging potential

Proximity to distribution networks can affect your business's success. If your business is capital-intensive such in aerospace, automotive, manufacturing or distribution you will incur higher costs of being closer to the bigger cities[33]. This will help you stay close to the market; however, you will need to ensure you are also close to your suppliers.

The cost of a location should include the sum of lease costs+ transport to market costs+ transport from suppliers + labour costs

If you have multiple location options available, all other factors being equal, you should aim to minimise the above cost. You may be able to negotiate a better deal with your suppliers if you are helping them save on transport costs.

If you have a product or service that requires a touch-and-feel experience, staying close to the market is important for your success. This will be relevant to apparel and cosmetics. Once you have a customer in the store to purchase such items (at least once), you may be able to take that customer online.

Staying close to a major market may impact operating costs or labour quality and cost; however, it may have a profound impact on logistics costs and therefore you will need to take into account all the likely costs that may be impacted by your choice of locations.

Depending on the size of the firm and the staff it employs, a dollar extra in labour costs would easily offset millions in transportation costs.

You should always aim to benchmark a site against other

---

[33] Bid rent theory explains how the price and demand of real estate changes as one moves further away from the CBD

sites. Though real-estate agents and consultants will offer you well-meaning advice, you should nevertheless make yourself comfortable with the decisions for the following reasons:

1. To identify the best purpose an asset can be put to
2. To help negotiate the best purchase or lease price;
3. To prospect the market potential of a location.

Currently, to establish the value of a real- estate asset, standard accounting practices prevail, which do not fully take into account the market potential. Taking into consideration a current and historical position as a lens to predict the future is great from a *status quo* point of view. Significant value creation of a real-estate asset occurs when its utilisation is well aligned with the market it serves.

Best utilisation of an asset at a location

When examining at an asset, creativity around how an asset is utilised plays a major role, equally significant to the market that it could serve. An asset can be restructured to incorporate multiple purposes that are all aligned with the market. This can be a case of subdividing, adding floors, or introducing vehicles and vans for delivery, which is the extension of the real estate itself.

In this case, core assets are a house in the main building and vehicles servicing the ancillary function. Uber food delivery is an example where the boundary of a real-estate asset is extended by marginally compromising food quality (temperature for hot foods).

The enormous value that is created by Uber delivery is primarily because it extends the restaurants to reach out to customers in a wider area.

While making real-estate decisions, we need to create a vision of the future, as there may be a demographic influx into or exodus from the area in question.

CHAPTER 6

Information as a key differentiator

Data and analytics relevant to the property where your business is located need to be well understood to make strategic decision. This data includes information on:

1. **Location:** The address where the store/business is located. By using a process called geocoding, this address can be turned into latitude and longitude. Latitude and longitude are coordinates on the Earth's surface. Using the latitude and longitude, every location on the spherical Earth can be placed on a map on a flat screen or on paper. Once the location is available, distances to other locations, direction, connectivity and containment (if one object is inside the other) can be established. This helps to ascertain how places are related physically and how they are likely to influence other locations.

2. **Floor area**: There are a number of terms you will encounter. Your focus needs to be on the area you can put to use for the intended purpose.

- **GLAR: Gross Leasable Area Retail**. For a shopping centre, this gives the size of the centre. The bigger the size, the more attractive it is likely to be.

- **Covered area**: The extent at ground level of the area of a building covered by one or more roofs, the perimeter of which (sometimes referred to as the drip line) is the outermost structural extension, this excludes ornamental overhangs

- **Floor area**: The area of a normally horizontal, permanent,
load-bearing structure, for each level of a building.

- **NLA**: Net lettable area. As this generates income, how it can be put to use impacts the bottom line.

- **Sheltered area**: Any part of a Covered Area that is not fully enclosed

3. **Rental**
- **Base rent**: The minimum rent due to the landlord, which is a fixed amount. This is a quoted, contracted amount of periodic rent. The annual base rate is the amount upon which escalations are calculated.

- **Fair market rent:** The rent that would normally be agreed upon by a willing landlord and tenant in an "arm's length transaction" for a specific property at a given time, even though the actual rent may be different. In a lease, the term "fair market rent" is defined in a number of different ways and is subject to extensive negotiation and interpretation.

4. **Availability:** When the property becomes available and for how long.

5. **Usage:** What purpose the asset can be used for.

6. **Frontage:** *Grunt from the front*– what is the visibility from the front? It also impacts the signage that can be used.

7. **Traffic** impacts the visibility and potential volume of customers. Traffic studies in an area may consist of the following:

- **Foot traffic:** Try and identify the following:
  - **Peak days**
  - **Traffic trends**
  - **Peak hours**
- **Traffic count with facial recognition**: There are a number of facial recognition software packages available that can count the foot or vehicular traffic. With recognition, you can differentiate whether the traffic is repeat traffic or not. You can flag the camera feed for VIP's.
- **Traffic count with MAC[34] addresses**: These are the addresses your computer or mobile devices have. If you have Apple or Google

---

[34] Media Access Control or MAC address is a unique numeric identifier. This numeric identifier is used to distinguish one device from aother in a network. This unique dddress is assigned by the manufacturer for ethernet and Wi-Fi cards.

phones/technologies, chances are that your location at any given point in time is being recorded. Once you are within the vicinity (fence) of a business or inside the floor area, this information (indicative) is available from, say, Google. You can also include your own sensors on the premises to run traffic counts. To extend it further you can create heat maps of the traffic movement in your premises to understand the preferences for a particular product on your shop floor or aisle.

- **Vehicular traffic:** This is available from your road and transport department. A number of providers have emerged who can provide you with the information using magnetic loops on the road, or sensing of MAC addresses.
- **AADT:** Annual average daily traffic helps benchmark the traffic on multiple roads
- **Peak traffic:** Reflects peak flow of traffic can help in estimating congestions.

Observing traffic that brings business

Your purpose should be to try and ascertain:

- How does the traffic change as the day goes by?
- When does the traffic peak during the day or night?
- Does the traffic pattern repeat itself every week?
- Is the traffic pattern impacted by school days?
- Is the traffic pattern impacted by holidays?
- Is the traffic pattern impacted by the snow season?

- Are there any festivals or events that change the traffic in the area?
- How does each type of vehicular traffic change over time? For example, the peak for cars may be seen around school pick-up and drop-off time, while trucks may be seen getting into the city early in the morning. You may want to check local laws. as it may vary from country to country, or even within the country it may vary significantly when you move to different areas or streets.
- You may like to review Google Traffic in your area.

Online Traffic

The challenge with online data is that it changes rapidly, but it can be easily measured by IP address. There are a number of service providers who can help you identify purchase history as well as propensity of a customer from an IP address (if online), or even pinpoint the location, demographics and psychographics.

Social Media

Social media has proliferated in our lives at a rapid rate. In the case of social media, the information about what happened, when it happened, who made it happen, who liked it and who shared it, is visible. Social media adheres to the principle of *kinship and followership*, which is a measure of likeability. When people are sharing information online and they have made their home location visible, it is very easy to cross-pollinate social media information from multiple sources and provide an integrated view of the customer.

CHAPTER 7

Information comes from data and data comes from everywhere

The sales performance of a store network depends on internal factors (sales area, staff experience, longevity), external factors that are site- specific (turnover at point of sales) and consumer-specific (catchment area, target group).

Someone who has been deeply entrenched in business, or a family that has been running through generations, builds gut feeling or rules of thumb that can be easily relied upon. These are akin to intellectual property that manifests gut feel. The only drawback with this is that it is vested internally and looks only to the past. It does not account for changes in market conditions, environment, competition, or disruption.

Anecdotally, irrespective of the size of the business, gut

feeling has led to tremendous Kodak moments (rapid decimation and extinction). This aspect is discussed in the next section on the loyalty card data. Customers, whether yours, your competitors', or those of any other collaborating business can contribute to create data.

A tremendous amount of data is being generated all around the globe, but only a fraction is captured and a much smaller fraction is analysed or visualised. The pipe keeps getting smaller and only a very tiny final universe of data is used in making any meaningful decisions in business.

Businesses that already see data as a way of differentiating between any external and outwardly mechanisms gain tremendous competitive advantage.

Important sources of customer information

- **Customer address:** This can be where they live, work, or on holiday. This information is provided by customers, or in online cases from their delivery address. If you are looking at delivering digital goods online, then it is an IP address.

- **Customer postal code:** In case customer's full address is not provided or is reluctant to share any personal information seeking post code is helpful. After establishing in Australia, IKEA asked for customer postcodes. Customer postcodes are a good mechanism to relate the type of products sold in an area. Relating purchase information between postcodes may not be very accurate to draw consumer level inferences. It helps in predicting the demand, particularly if an area is recording growth or exhibiting an influx of population in correlation with growth in product sales.

- **Purchase information from the customer:** A number of firms buy the barcode data from the supermarket checkouts and are able to analyse the items sold and run a basket correlation. For example, if you buy bread, then you are likely to buy milk. This helps in cross-promoting products and hence increase profitability per customer.

- **Total basket:** This is used to compare the total basket between locations and between businesses and determine what customers are buying and where. This, when correlated with the demographics and psychographics of the market a business serves, gives an understanding of consumption patterns, tastes and preferences. This may include information such as whether a customer who buys a product A is then likely to buy product B; or whether if they buy product A they are unlikely to buy product B. This can be used to cross-promote products

Understand business trends using data based on

- purchase dates: trends around Christmas or Easter;
- purchase by time of day;
- products purchased;
- specials: To depict price sensitivity, who are these price- sensitive customers. What are they price-

sensitive to?

- customer promiscuity;
- brand promiscuity;
- demographic profiling;
- pricing over location: how pricing shifts over a geographic area;
- Loyalty pricing of products: how loyal customers have to be incentivised to enhance the overall business value.

Understanding some of the trends above becomes easier with the use of loyalty information.

Reasons to acquire, store, manage and track customer loyalty data

The value of loyalty card data cannot be underestimated if you are in the retail business. Here are a few reasons why:

Reason 1: Customer retention

According to Bain and Co., a 5% increase in customer retention can increase a company's profitability by 75%.
Loyalty programs create a basis to help customers to continue to buy. The accumulated reward points can help them seek higher levels of service. The information received about customers helps in meeting their needs efficiently, effectively and engagingly.
The symbiotic process creates a lock-in and helps customers

remain with business. The energy starts building once the customers start redeeming points.

The data generated by loyalty program helps in segmenting customers for sales, marketing and customer service. Customers' needs and desires vary based on time, location, occasion, destination and intention.

Reason 2: Customer acquisition

Once the cycle of redeeming rewards is initiated by an existing customer, the value appropriated thus creates a voice or a signal that works like a reference. Robert Cialdini refers to it as *social proof*. Customers start creating word of mouth. This word of mouth creates a follow-on effect that brings more interested prospects through the door. You need to make sure you have the mechanisms and reasons for existing entrenched and happy customers to broadcast the fact.

Birds of a feather flock together, so rewarding the existing market will lead to word of mouth in the target market provided your targeting is correct.

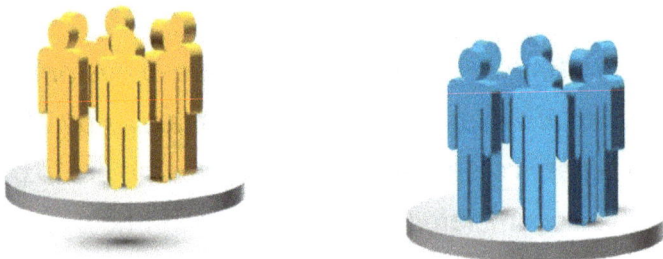

If you need to go up, down, or sideways in the propensity, then in addition to nurturing existing customers, upselling, discounting or cross-selling opportunities must be looked at respectively. Data is used to identify the demographic and psychographic lookalike segments of existing ideal customers who fit the criteria as a starting point.

Reason 3: Competing with self and laddering up

Get the customers to move up tiers and as they move up, they unlock a new set of bands of reward segments. This is very similar to how most video games work. Their ability to unlock greater benefits compels them to create a better version of themselves and for the business.

This is often linked to increased spending or spending on particular goods or services within a timeframe. If needed make it location-specific by building traffic to a new location that has just opened up. Though it should not be your primary purpose (and may be illegal in your country), as gift cards usually have an expiry date on them and if not used within a timeframe, customers may not be able to redeem them, you may end up collecting cash upfront for goods or services that you may not ever provide.

Reason 4: Retire unwanted customers.

These are the customers that you don't want or need. They are unprofitable, waste your time, complain without reason and create a bad brand image. You need to retire them immediately (keep the book aside and do it now), as losing them will create room within your business to go out and acquire new ones. Some call it cherry-picking; we call it well segmented. You may very well send them to your competition. Your loyalty program should reward good customers and not the bad ones. A simple way to measure it is to have a scoring criterion measuring the degree of bad experiences with the customers in conjunction with their potential lifetime value[35].

Your loyalty data will indicate whether the lifetime value or satisfaction is going up for that particular customer. Should both be going down and your business has nothing to do with it (*Note: if your business has everything to do with it then loss of customers is inevitable and immediate investigation is warranted*), you should consider retiring them. (This is very simplistic and real analysis will need to dig deeper.)

Designing a loyalty program that rewards better customers without rewarding the bad segment will certainly show unwanted ones the door.

Philip Kotler's adaptation of the Pareto principle suggests that the top 20% of customers generate 80% of the profits, while the bottom 30% of customers eat up 50% of the profits that the others produce. That is a good reason why you should aim to eliminate, sack, or fire dud customers.

Reason 5: Win back customers.

Once you have information on a customer in your database (their address, their demographic and psychographic profile), it is easier to reach out to them if they have not visited your business for a while.

It is easier to reach out to them after they have shopped with. It is relatively difficult to entice unknown prospects into your business.

---

[35] How Valuable are your customers; Amy Gallo HBR, July 15, 2014

However, if customers are not responding to you via existing channels you may try other options such as sending coupons or offers electronically instead of using snail mail (if you have not tried this earlier). This option is also helpful if the customers have moved to a different geographic location and are unable to shop at the usual location.

You should consider servicing relocated customers via an online platform, or if you have a large number of customers co-located in a new area, you should consider establishing a new outlet depending on the critical mass of prospects for your new establishment. A conversation with a pizza shop owner who expressed his frustration to me that most of his customers came from a pocket few kilometres away and how it is causing delivery nightmares (those were pre-Uber days) I suggested that he should consider selling his current business and starting a new business somewhere near the location causing him delivery nightmares. Result: his business at new location was a stellar success. He made a tidy sum of profit by selling the existing business and reinvesting proceeds in the new business. He was running an independent shop, so he was able to leverage his personal relationship and brand at this new location.

Reason 6: Creating sneezers

As Seth Godin[36] would put it, these are champions who promote your offerings, exhibiting the highest form of loyalty. They infect others with their passion for your products or

---

[36] https://sethgodin.typepad.com/seths_blog/files/2000Ideavirus.pdf

services. A measure net promoter score[37] is something you should look for if you want to measure the willingness of your existing customers to recommend products and services to new prospects.

These sneezers infect others, or in other words, they are so passionate about the products or services received from you that they are overwhelmed and will go around telling others, thus promoting your product. Amway uses multilevel marketing via this mechanism. It does not replace the natural level of enthusiasm a passionate customer may bring, but it does work. While you make up your mind about a particular product or service to buy, a close friend's recommendation is extremely likely to sway your opinion.

Reason 7: Select new trading sites.

Many businesses still select a new site for a store by sticking a pin in the map and/or then closing the stores that are underperforming. This can be a significant drain on infrastructure, resources and the mojo of the company.
Selecting a new store location can be done easily by using loyalty card data. It enables you to identify the profile and demographics   of existing best customers and then find the demographic and psychographic lookalike for new locations.
Additionally, if the addresses of existing customers are known, they can be plotted geographically and a new location can be identified where there are large numbers not served

---

[37] The one number you need to grow, by Frederick F. Reichheld. *HBR*, December 2003

by existing stores.

Reason 8: Managing pricing

If a reasonable number of your best customers are willing to buy a product at a price, then reducing the price further simply suggests you are attracting occasional cherry-pickers, who may not be entrenched enough to give you an ongoing revenue stream. With loyalty card data it is easy to find established customers and their willingness to pay[38] based on past purchases or discounts. This information can be drilled down to customer segments and hence the most profitable pricing for a product or service can be set.

Reason 9: Competitive response

Using the loyalty data, it is easy to link purchases to customers and then identify the customers who are likely to move to new competition (churn analysis is a common term used for the process). They can be lured back by providing customer-specific special offers.

Using loyalty data, it is easy to differentiate between regular shoppers and others and incentivise regular shoppers via mail or electronically when a new competition opens up and starts operating in the area.

Reason 10: Enhancing Customer Lifetime Value

In the simplest terms, the profit from each customer should be

---

[38] How to find out what customers will pay, by Rafi Mohammed. *HBR*, September 2012

more than the cost of acquiring them. It is the calculation of net profit from a customer during the entirety of the relationship. In mathematical terms, it is the net present value of projected future cash flows from business from a given customer. Retaining customers and getting them to keep coming back, getting them to buy more and buy often is part of the game.

As an example, if a business loses 30% of its customers each month and does not acquire any new customers, in 12 months they will have no customers; hence there should be an impetus on customer satisfaction. That said, not all businesses (consider funeral homes) may expect repeat sales at the pace of online platforms, but the service should not be compromised as it creates an ongoing word of mouth.

An enhanced customer lifetime value, or CLV, will increase the value of your business.

Customer Retention

Reason 11: Best customer marketing

This concept simply suggests identifying the best customers

and then spending energy, time, money and resources on the best customers to maximise your return on investment. You can then look at moving the customers who are not the best (but with not far from the best customer criteria), into the best customer pool, or alternatively, stop serving them if they are at the bottom rung. This may sound like a ruthless approach, but it pays to serve your best customers and make room to invite other best customers into the market. *Let your customers earn the right to be served by you.*

Reason 12: Effective stock selection

This entails keeping the stock in line with what the best customers buy frequently and expanding on those lines. When you align the stock to the most profitable customers, the entire store becomes more appealing to your best customers and to prospects who are similar to your best customers. It is a slow process but is a combination of inviting best customer lookalikes in conjunction with self-exclusion of customers who don't fit your best customer category.

Some businesses do have a nasty habit of sending their loss-making, angry or irate customers to the competition, so be mindful when you see this game being played, as this can be a significant drain on your energy and resources.

In terms of stocking, you can gradually remove the lines that your best customers don't prefer and add the lines they do and gradually your business will be shaped in line with the market you wish to serve. It includes all the steps you take to serve your best customer. The Louis Vuitton shop, with the security at the entrance and a queue that only allows a certain number of prospects in the shop; makes its prospects feel elated and privileged just to enter the business premises. This works as a filter to keep out those who are unlikely to buy, but the sense of privilege boosts the willingness to pay for those who may be sitting on the fence.

Reason 13: Relationships

The most successful businesses reduce the friction between the customer and the transaction, irrespective of the type of business (online or offline). This reduction in friction simplifies the customer's journey with you. The simplified journey feeds the energy back into building the relationship and increases bottom-line profits. If the customer tries to move to another provider, the increased friction of transaction elsewhere will bring them back to you. You will have come across the saying, "It's not what you know, it's who you know." The purpose here is to reduce the transactional friction and de-risk the transaction by dealing with someone you already know.

(Image courtesy slidemodel.com)

You need to choose who you want to build a relationship with. Attempting to partner with all customers regardless of their characteristics might not always be the best way forward, as you may end up choosing dead weight.

Reason 14: Merchandise planning

When you run a basket analysis for a set of customers you can identify lines or products bought at the same time and in particular by your best customers. Planograms (placement of products in 3D) can be planned accordingly to encourage cross-purchasing. Basket analysis without any loyalty program will suffice for this purpose.

However, once you include the dimensions of knowing who the customer is, what their spend is and where they live, work or travel, you can confidently decide whether it is worth putting on a display of items that are bought together by a specific segment of the market on a specific day of the week.

Reason 15: Optimising spend on promotion

Moving on to targeted advertising, instead of "spraying and praying, laser-sharp targeting of customers can be done down to a category of one. Instead of sending out thousands of flyers, of which a significant chunk is chucked away, or newspaper ads that are skipped over as being irrelevant, targeted advertising reaches out to individual customers and provides tailor-made offers (think WIIFM – What's in it for me from customer's perspective).

This can be done via email based on past sales to the

customer. The more sophisticated type of loyalty program can target advertising material almost individually to its many millions of members and can accurately measure the response rates to those advertisements. Should your customers also be online, you can use tools from companies like *Digital Element* to tailor your entire website based on customers' preference and past purchases. Furthermore, you can use their IP address to identify their location or shopping behaviour with the utmost precision.

Reason 16: Providing Loyalty as currency.

Ability to trade the loyalty points as currency, and letting the customers trade the points with friend's results in creating a marketplace. Creating a constrainted and transparent marketplace helps bring more people in the fold. Qantas airlines in Australia allows transferring the points to family members. It allows you to earn bonus points as an incentive when you sign up for credit cards, energy or with cross promoting other products.

Obtaining loyalty card data

Your customers can become part of a loyalty scheme, following which they can pay by card or cash. It is easy to know what was in your customer's basket today, yesterday, or last year and how the purchases have trended over time. You can understand the trend in consumption of toilet rolls and correlate that with the purchase of the spicy sauce and have a fair guess that the overseas guests have arrived. Tesco has the ability to using its Clubcard database and make you eat healthily by offering you vouchers of salad and fruit.

For each loyalty point you award your customers, you can collect a huge amount of information about their shopping habits. These can be leveraged in many different ways in addition to providing very targeted offers.

You can understand whether a particular customer responds better to vouchers or pays by credit, debit cards, or cash.

If your customers are part of a loyalty program, you can build up their demographic and psychographic profile: what they buy, how much they spend, where they live and how they are distributed geographically. In conjunction with their distribution, you can identify the ideal demographic and psychographic conditions where they are ought to be found but are missing. You may just find gaps in the market and market in the gaps using this strategy.

If your store is online and customers buy from a physical location, you can identify the psychographics and demographics of customers in near-real time based on their location or past purchase history and filter the content to their preferred past purchases.

A number of financial institutions are now interested in selling the data they hold in an anonymised and tokenised format, which is now used to identify the area customers live in and the purchase they have made. Due to privacy reasons, the customers may not be identifiable; however, over a broader region it is easy to identify the pattern and trends to the extent that you can identify the fingerprint of consumption in an area (based on the percent of consumption in different categories) and then extrapolate that to find lookalikes that may be good for your expansion strategy.

Tesco targets its 16 million Clubcard holders via targeted ads using a free movie service. The data for targeting is obtained from the purchasing behaviour. It is equally easy to target customers using online purchases and credit card data. If you are an Amazon Prime member and get to watch unlimited movies perhaps you are sharing your preferences likes and dislikes.

The effectiveness of promotions is now measured by the number of unique card transactions that emerge due to a specific event or promotion.

The common practice in the retail industry is that card numbers are not connected to an individual or an address, hence supermarkets encourage customers to acquire cards with their own store branding that offer extra incentives, while customers exchange valuable information and so strengthening the two-way relationship.

The supermarkets also want to find out what their customers are doing outside their stores. I helped an organisation that used "market information "about shoppers to decide on new store locations.

Anonymised, aggregated information about what we are all spending on our credit and debit cards and where we are spending it is potentially up for grabs from providers like Data Republic.

Visa says it requires its issuing banks to seek your agreement when you apply for its card. MasterCard states, in its global privacy policy, that it will "perform data analyses" and offers you the chance to opt out on its website; otherwise, you are automatically opted in.

Both Visa and MasterCard emphasise that they do not share your personal details, such as your name and address. However, it is still possible to monitor what you buy and identify products which, when scanned-in at the checkout, act as "triggers" for the cashiers to hand over different types of incentives.

Coupons at checkouts are used to target cash-paying customers. It is simply a matter of identifying consumers whose buying preferences match a particular product.

Other types of market data

Several other significant types of market data are available to aid your business (depending on the country in which you are working). These include the following:

- Businesses (classified to categories) in a postcode (or any defined geographic boundary) area that fall into a category.

- Stores that are opening or closing.

- Sometimes only sample data and demographic information are available. Using techniques like simulation modelling, this can be extrapolated to the

143

entire market.

- You can analyse media/advertisement spend information to understand the effort being undertaken by your competitors.
- Significant data nowadays available from banks and card companies or through data brokerage platforms.
- Other sources of market data can include the following:
  - Proprietary surveys or tracking studies
  - Proprietary databases/software
  - Omnibus surveys
  - Government agencies and departments
  - Government statistics
  - Professional/industry associations/employer associations
  - Census data
  - Observed purchase behaviours
  - Data-mining techniques
  - Commissioned research

Business data and associated statistics may have the following benchmarks to relate to industry standards:

Key Measurements

Measuring performance

- **Sales per square foot/metre**: This is the most commonly used type of data. It can be used to calculate return on investment and thus rent, on a retail location. When measuring sales per square foot/metre, you should ensure that the selling space does not include the stockroom or any area where products are not displayed. The purpose here is to take net utilisable space in consideration.

Sales per square foot/metre of selling space = total net sales ÷ square feet/metre of selling space

- **Sales per linear foot/metre of shelf space:** A retail store

  with wall units and other shelf space may want to use sales per linear foot/metre of shelf space to determine a product or product category's allotment of space.

  Sales per linear foot/metre = total net sales ÷ linear feet/metre of shelving

Measuring performance of inventory

- **Sales by department or product category:** Retailers selling various categories of products will find the sales by department tool useful in comparing product categories within a store.

  Category's % of total store sales = category's total net sales ÷ store's total net sales

The biggest drain on your cash is your inventory in a retail business. Measuring your turnover is one way to know if you are overstocked or even under-stocked on an item. You can extend it further to assess the % profit and % area covered by the category in question to establish if a particular category (or product helps in your bottom line in a positive or negative

145

manner)

Measuring productivity of staff

Also known as sales per customer, the **sales per transaction** figure tells a retailer the average transaction in dollars. A store dependent on its salespeople to make a sale will use this formula in measuring the productivity of staff.

Sales per transaction = gross sales ÷ number of transactions

When factoring **sales per employee**, you need to take into consideration whether the store has full-time or part-time workers. Convert the hours worked by part-time employees during the period to an equivalent number of full-time workers. This form of measuring productivity is an excellent tool for determining the number of sales a business needs to generate when increasing staffing levels.

Sales per employee = net sales ÷ number of employees

As a retailer, you need to track these numbers month by month and year by year. As you do, it becomes easier to understand where the sales are generated, by which employees and how the store's merchandising can maximise sales growth.

Break-even analysis

This is the point in your retail business where sales equal expenses; there is no profit and no loss. For example, for a retail store, rent is likely to be the same regardless of the number of units sold.

> *Break-even ($) = fixed costs ÷ gross marginal percentage*

Cost of goods sold

This is the price paid for a product, plus any additional costs necessary to get the merchandise into inventory and ready for sale, including shipping and handling. In some cases, pilferage and damage may need to be taken into consideration.

Gross margin

This is simply the difference between what an item costs and the price at which it sells.

Initial mark-up

Initial mark-up (IMU) is a calculation to determine the selling price   a retailer puts on an item in his store. Some of the things that affect initial mark-up are brand, competition, market saturation, anticipated markdowns and perceived customer value, to name a few.

> *Initial mark-up % = (expenses + reductions + profit)*
> *÷ (net sales + reductions)*

Margin

This is the amount of gross profit a business earns when an item is sold.

Net sales

Net sales are the amount of sales generated by a business after the deduction of returns, allowances for damaged or missing goods and any discounts allowed.

Net sales = gross sales - returns and allowances

Other data analysis methods

- You may like to collect and manage customer transaction records, e.g., sale value per transaction, purchase frequency
- Patron membership records, e.g., active members, lapsed members, length of membership
- Customer relationship management (CRM) databases to track interaction
- In-house surveys
- Customer self-completed questionnaires or feedback forms

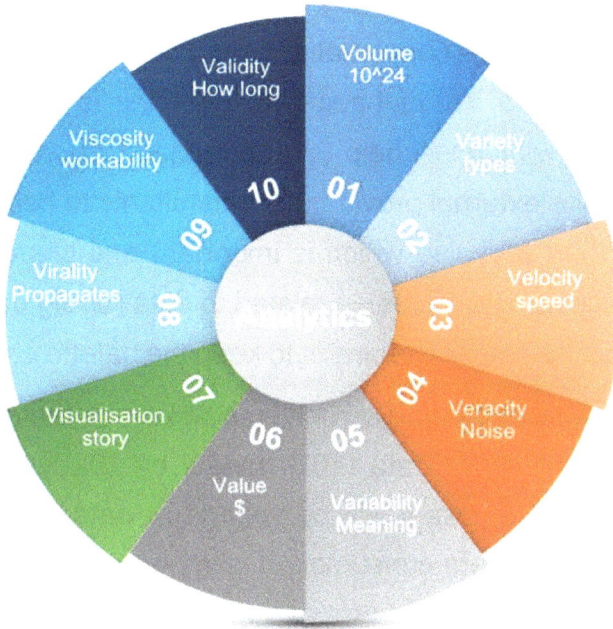

Vs in the world of data

When you hear the conversations on data you will also hear about V's of data. Without going too deep this is going to be a quick primer which will help you understand the nuances. In case you hire external providers or consultants to help you out you can then prioritise which is important and significant for your business. The variables related to data (or big data) start with V and the purpose seems is to keep the palette consistent.

- **Volume:** The digital universe will reach more than 40 zettabytes of data (1024 bytes) by 2020. In case of your business it will be volume of data produced or external data consumed. It is important to understand from storage and processing point of view

- **Velocity:** Speed and the direction the data is coming from is rapidly increasing. It is happening because of the sheer increase in volume and connectivity. How quickly you will need to make decisions?

- **Variety:** Type of datasets very significantly, from traditional documents and databases to semi-structured, unstructured data, GPS locations, social media pictures and IOT (internet of things). Combining them together creates a whole new meaning. Do you need weather information in conjunction with school holiday information? Or you need city event information with roads closed and nearest parking information. Each data comes in its own structure. To be able to combine variety of data from multiple sources can give your business the needed edge.

- **Veracity**: The noise, abnormality or bias in data. It is separating the relevant from irrelevant.

- **Variability**: Data where the meaning is constantly changing. For example, the same words may be present in a different context. Are you logging customer complaint calls? The context of the conversation will determine what the client is complaining about. Sometimes it is not about what they say but what they interpret to have occurred.

- **Value:** The value that can be created by the use of data. This can be subjective based on data workflows and knowledge and skills and technologies available to create such value. Are you able to monetise the data that you create?

- **Visualisation:** A picture is worth a thousand words. When it comes to data, (static, or dynamic data) it can be used to tell a story in a coherent, conceivable and communicable way.

- **Virality**: How the data spreads among other users and applications? Social media is known to make or break businesses.

- **Viscosity**: How difficult it is to work with the data.

- **Validity/Volatility**: How long the data is valid for and how long it should be stored. In the real-time world what happened a month ago may not have relevance for analysis today.

Analytics

Big data analytics is the process of examining large and varied data sets — i.e., big data — to uncover hidden patterns, unknown correlations, market trends, customer preferences and other useful information that can help organisations make more informed business decisions.

Data provides facts including preferences and bias. Sometimes segmenting the market and measuring consumer behaviour gives great feedback, which allows tailoring of the product or shaping the marketing to what consumers prefer.

Adore Me, a fast-fashion lingerie company that has experienced tremendous growth, used data and artificial intelligence to learn about consumers on a large scale. This allows them to tailor their marketing strategy.

They run A/B testing on lingerie models through an A/B testing platform. For each set of lingerie, they shoot multiple versions of images to run on our website. The difference between two images might be as simple as the model having her hand on her hip or in her hair. For every 1,000 people who come to their website, 500 will see picture A and 500 picture B — they then see which images shoppers click on more and hence which one leads to more sales.

(Source: Business Insider)

Case Study: Bias

Image Courtesy Utpal Dholakia
(George R. Brown Professor of Marketing at Rice University)

There is a bias of 35% in the above picture as women's deodorant was at 35% premium. There can be multiple reasons for this ranging from pink tax (higher prices for women's products than comparable men's products)

Other reasons include versioning, formulation, who is the actual buyer of the product (different price sensitivity), different demand levels for men and women which leads to a price difference (more you need, more you are willing to pay). Is the product introduced in the market is at a different stage of lifecycle (showing different levels of traction and brand presence) Perhaps I will extend it to different demographic regions and also see if the price bias is consistent But it could also be someone just thought if this number as a good number to start things off then tweak it in the time to come. Irrespective of what the correct answers is the bias continues to dominate and as a business owner you will need to understand if you need to create a bias that works for you.

Factors affecting the success of a business

As discussed before, the success of a business depends on some or all of the following factors being favourable:

1. **Reach:** (How are we responding to distinct groups, or how are the distinct groups reaching us?)
2. **Message:** (What is our message to our market? Is the market able to take some actions on the message that helps in creating value? Are they listening to us? Do they understand us?
3. **Market:** (Identifying distinct groups within the market, the characteristics of those groups, how big those groups are, etc.)

Now it is easy to reach out to the category of one individual due to the advent of technology. However, to optimise the efforts it is easier to club the customers together into groups, categories, or technically speaking, market segments. This can be done based on

Person> personality> behaviour> location> group/household> environment

Or

Demographic> psychographics> consumption> geographic> situation

The need to ask questions if data is not available

Market research is a way of getting an overview of consumers' wants, needs and beliefs. It can also involve discovering how they   act. The research is used to determine how a product will be marketed. Peter Drucker believed market research to be the quintessence of marketing. Market research is a way in which producers and the marketplace study the consumer and gather information about the consumer's needs. There are two major types of market research: **Primary research**, which is sub-divided into qualitative research and quantitative research; and **secondary research**.

Factors that can be investigated through market research include:

- **Market information:** Using market information, one can know the prices of different commodities in the market, as well as the supply and demand situation. Market researchers have a wider role than previously recognised by helping their clients to understand social, technical and even legal aspects of markets.

- **Market segmentation** is the division of the market or population into subgroups with similar motivations. It is widely used for segmenting on geographic differences, demographic differences (age, gender, ethnicity, etc.), technographic differences (consumers based on their ownership, use patterns and attitudes toward information, communication and entertainment technologies), psychographic differences (personality, values, opinions, attitudes, interests and lifestyles) and differences in product use. For B2B segmentation firmographics (SIC codes, company size, location) is commonly used.

- **Market trends** are the upward or downward

movement of a market, over a period of time. Determining the market size may be more difficult if one is starting with a new innovation. In this case, you will have to derive the figures from the number of potential customers or customer segments.

- **SWOT** is a written analysis of the Strengths, Weaknesses, Opportunities and Threats of a business entity. A SWOT analysis helps to develop the marketing and product mixes. Another factor that can be measured is marketing effectiveness (how effective a given marketer's strategy is toward meeting the goal of maximising their spending to achieve positive results in both the short and long term).

Market research may include the following:

- Customer analysis (Segmentation of target customers)
- Choice modelling
- Competitor analysis
- Risk analysis
- Product research
- Advertisement research
- Marketing mix modelling
- Simulated test marketing.

Look around and you may get a plethora of information including:

City planning: You can gain rich information on the existing conditions, land use and the plans that will affect the city in the future. This is a good resource on infrastructure, movement of population, etc. An understanding of this gives a reflection of the current impetus and leveraging opportunities that may present themselves.

Growth corridors: Areas that are earmarked for growth. Sometimes there are areas where people from a specific country of origin or ethnicity come together. This impacts the purchase preferences in an area.

Transport network: Especially   if a new transport infrastructure is planned, as usually new suburbs, cities and human establishment establish around such networks. Depending on the volume of traffic flow likely, commercial opportunities that may emerge can be easily anticipated.

Living population vs working population: People usually
live in suburban areas and then travel to a commercial part of the city to work. This reflects the demand on road infrastructure. There is increased demand for products and services that cater to this working population near their work. During the non-work hours certain business activities are deeply marginalised.

Long-distance traffic: The areas through which the long-distance traffic passes gives immense opportunities for drive-by shopping. You will see an agglomeration of businesses near gas stations that offer food, shopping and entertainment. Providing toilet facilities or free food for drivers gives an additional bonus point for the traffic to be pulled in.

Walk around the town: Try and walk around the town with a notebook in your hand and observe the traffic, the business, the crowds, what is doing well and what is not. It gives a lens, an insight into any opportunities that are still unexploited.

CHAPTER 8

Ingredients of your Secret Sauce

Your recipe of success can have few or too many ingredients, however they have to come together in a cohesive, consistent and consequential way.

Ingredient: Traffic

Customers are the reason any business exists. Traffic (online, mobile or physical) is key is what brings customers and builds traction. This traction builds your sales funnel and takes customers and prospects on a journey. Like a bag of popped corn some are likely to bounce off and some are not fit for consumption, likewise not all traffic is relevant or will bring business and perhaps some may cause toothache. You may need to pick the best ones.

A measure of traffic being good or bad in your proximity

depends on its motivation to be in your area (besides shopping).

- **Price matching**: These are buyers who are checking out new products or services to see how much they will cost. Their opportunity cost of time is usually low, so engaging with them may be counterproductive.

- **Shoplifting**: Ensure your policy allows you to check bags, have cameras, security with valuable items secure under lock and key. Be wary of kleptomaniacs[39] who pick things just for the sake of it.

- **Bargaining**: Better than price-matchers, they will buy if the price is right, but make sure you have strategies to convert them without spending too much energy on them.

- **Window shopping**: Curious bystanders who want to see what is out there and at what price. Don't underestimate this category as they may have the ability to not only buy the most expensive products or services that money can buy, this group can include investors or individuals looking to acquire/invest in your business.

- **Waiting**: These are just waiting for another activity initiate by themselves or someone associated to be completed (family member shopping, car being serviced, etc.). Mostly they are bored, but lure them in and you never know, you may have a customer for life.

---

[39] Kleptomania is characterized by recurrent episodes of compulsive stealing. Stealing commonly occurs in the form of shoplifting. The items involved are usually of trivial value and are not needed by the individual stealing them.
Kleptomania and Potential Exacerbating Factors, Innovations in clinical neuroscience 2011 Oct; 8(10): 35–39. Published online 2011 Oct. A Review and Case Report, Farid Ramzi Talih, MD

A OnePoll survey suggests that US women spend 50+ hours each year window-shopping

Ingredient2: Origin and evolution of traffic

Since time immemorial, transportation networks have laid the foundations of commerce, which has helped to establish the cities and the businesses within. Each town has a symbiotic relationship with its transport networks. The spread of the town and the associated transport hubs have helped the business grow.

The traffic that helps the business can be living traffic that lives in the vicinity of business, or working traffic consisting of those who come to an area for professional purposes. The third type of traffic that may exist an area can be passing-through traffic, which is there just temporarily.

Ingredient 3: Traffic attractors

Land uses such as the following pull traffic into an area:
- Fetes or exhibitions
- Petrol stations
- Schools
- Public transport access
- Train stations, airports, traffic hubs
- Shops or eateries
- Tourist spots
- Offices
- Religions places

- Cinemas
- Hospitals
- Banks

A Harvard study[40] found that clustering (when one or more of these centres are co-located) tends to tip the balance for an area to become a destination. Increased traffic even at the cost of extra competition leads to businesses benefit. Extra competition weeds out the underperformers and hence customers and businesses both benefit.

Ingredient 4: Traffic detractors

This should be deliberately avoided. Construction activity, heavy accidents, noise, bad smells, lack of activity and empty and abandoned buildings (which create a sense of fear and uncertainty) can all take traffic away from an area.

If you have a physical store you may also like to look at some physical attributes that can move traffic away from you; for example:

- Closed doors or access from unlikely doors
- Too many steps (Old people may resent coming back again.)
- Too many things on the path to the inside that detract, such as your big policy statement that says damages must be paid for fragile objects along the way. Forget having families with kids adorning your store!

Ingredient 5: Healthy Competition

[40] Clusters and new economises of competition, by Michael E Porter. *HBR*. December 1998

Competitors lead to a level of cannibalisation and decline of business, but in the long run, a healthy level of competition is good, as it results in bringing out the best via differentiation. Competitors will compete, but if they are in close proximity, they bring more business into an area. Too many competitors in an area will invariably result in formation of an association or guild.

I am sure you would know a street in your town that is popular for a particular type of food. Businesses in such areas compete, but it pulls traffic from other areas. This is commonly known as *co-opetition*.[41]

Businesses compete with each other, but many similar businesses when co-located, generate traffic for each other from a greater distance away. A general practice and a pharmacist located next to each other is an ideal example. Another example would be a butcher and a bakery located close by, each of which helps the other's business. Hence in such a situation you should consider offering reciprocal opportunities.

Ingredient6: Traffic exterminators

This is an ingredient that should be deliberately avoided if you can, as they can completely destroy the business in an area. These may not be permanent but of a defined or predictable duration. You can also explore alternatives when traffic

---

[41] Co-Opetition, Business and Economics, by Adam M. Brandenburger and Barry J. Nalebuff: Crown Business

exterminators are in play in an area

New traffic routes that make it easier for traffic that once went past the front of your business may lead to a decline in traffic.

Based part of the world you are in, there can be varied traffic exterminators at work. Sometimes, they may work in your favour. For example, a royal motorcade going on a stretch of a road, sporting activity, or construction activity that has stopped the movement of traffic, results in one of the following two scenarios:

- The traffic finds a different route and travels on it and thus the detractor may result in the loss of business.
- The traffic comes to a standstill for a reasonable time, which then results in discretionary spending in the vicinity.

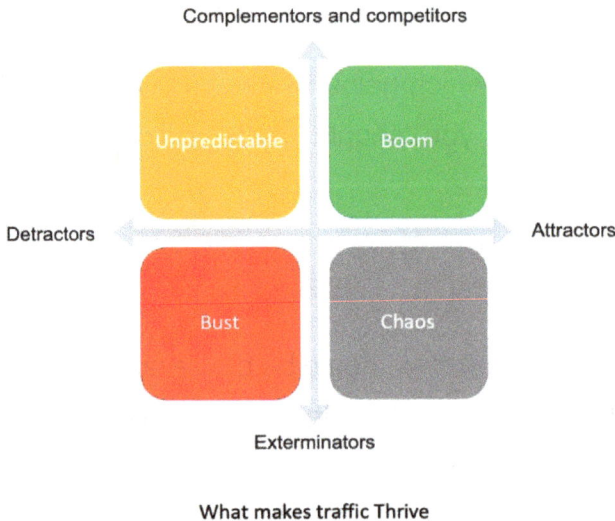

What makes traffic Thrive

The diagram above summarises the likely business outcome based on how the ingredients play out.

164

CHAPTER 9

Cannibalisation is good and bad

Investment in real estate is the most expensive commitments any business can make, be it a lease or a buy decision. When scaling up or franchising, every business is ambitious to reach the best market penetration possible. That means focus should be on installing stores that are close to the market.

In the high-consumption and high-propensity areas, customers are spoilt for choice; and when too much choice is available to the customers, they end up shopping in multiple locations.

Illusion of choice: Image courtesy Alexander S Pervushin. You may think you are clever in doing maths and pick up two shaving gel's instead of a twin pack. In a crowded market place it is bound to get your attention.

Say the willingness of a customer to travel to get to a store or a type of store is 3 km and he has two stores available within 3 km, then the chances are that the customer may optionally switch between the two stores. The combined revenue of these stores from this particular customer provides only half the benefit to each of the stores over a long period of time.

If such a possibility is available to 5,000 such customers to conveniently shop at either of two locations, then the customers may be split between the two stores.

A similar analysis can be done by combining the data from customers who shop at both locations.

Data available to identify this may include bank transaction data, credit card data (which is usually anonymised and tokenised to depict the region they are from) apportioning to a smaller geographic area.

Continuing with the above example, if the above 5,000 customers have an annual spending on grocery of, say, $5,000, then between the two stores $2.5 m/2, or $1.25 m annually, is wasted by locating them close by as these customers could have shopped at either of the locations.

That said, do customers have a willingness to drive to buy groceries at a maximum of 3 km away, then if you install the outlets that may require a travel of up to 4 km, you may end up missing out some customers. Hence careful planning is needed to install stores.

Some of the scenarios to think

- if the part of the city is rapidly expanding and more options to shop are becoming available. Over time, the willingness of customers to travel the distance will decline as they will start experiencing greater friction due to traffic, parking and other factors which will impact their decisions.

- people living in sparsely populated areas, the willingness to travel a greater distance may be intrinsically higher as driving at higher speeds they may be able to reach the destination quicker.

The most commonly used model for sales analysis is the gravity model. A simplistic way to explain would be via the diagram of sales versus the distance at which customers live below, you will notice that sales are higher from customers who live close to the outlet and it declines as the distance increases. The maximum distance where customers can come from is infinity (far end off the planet). An example of this is to note that a potential customer can be one who is visiting from interstate or overseas.

This model is prevalent in the case of bricks-and-mortar stores that sell

commodity items. The area under the curve suggests the sales

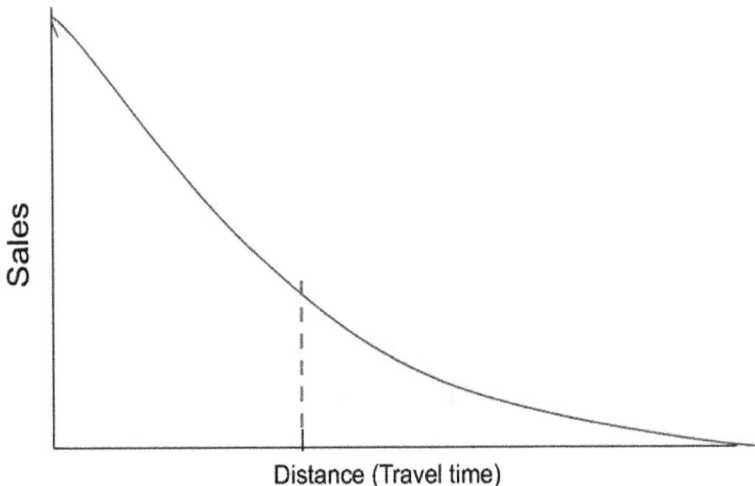

Distance (Travel time)

occurring at the store.

Let's fast forward the discussions to a competitive environment. If the business is attractive, then it will bring competition.

The area under the curve will most likely resemble the curve above if plotted for a shop. Simply suggesting that the distance from which customers come to the business greater the distance lesser the revenue. This does not apply to online business however cost of logistics including the last mile is

considered.

In a perfect world, we may find a formula that will help us find

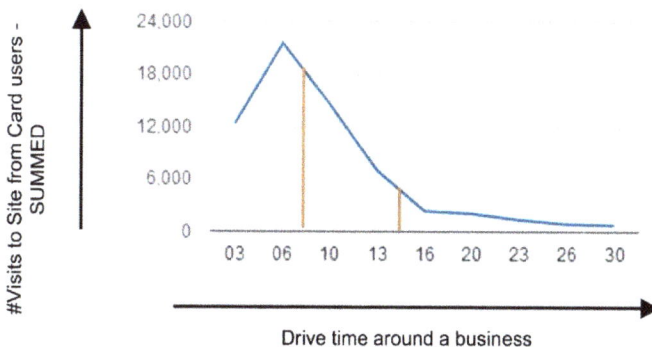

169

the impact of competition, but it may not be the case, so we will resort to more practical and simplistic means.

In a group or a chain, we will first find the businesses that are in a similar demographic lookalike scenario. We look for market look alikes.

We identify the sales that are coming from the customers from different distances. (Ideally, we can use travel time or travel distance as a variable.) I would strongly discourage drawing concentric rings, because though it is an easy exercise, it can be extremely misleading as it ignores the true spread and concentration of population. You may hire a consultant who knows how to run this exercise using gravity models and traveling salesmen models or you may try and do it yourself

There are a number of free and extremely low-cost software programs that you can use for the purpose of plotting the customers on the map and identifying how far they are coming from. If you are looking for a free GIS solution, I can recommend QGIS (I can confirm that I am not getting any benefit from QGIS for this recommendation).

Looking at the above figure, it appears that the revenue contribution of customers with up to 3 minutes of travel time is about $12,000, then for a distance of 6-minute drive time it is $22,000. This falls to $7,000 at 13 minutes and $2,000 at 16 minutes.

Complex mathematical analysis can be done in this case to calculate the market potential in each case; however, this simpler method will give an excellent indicative representation.

Markets are generally lucrative when high competitive intensity is matched with higher-category spending.

For a well-defined business model, if the category spending is higher (or in other words, a business is getting a disproportionately higher- category spending), the likelihood of competitive intensity to grow in the catchment is higher. If it continues to grow beyond sustainable levels, then the following may occur:

- Either one or more of the businesses start underperforming, have their profits squeezed, or exit the market.
- The attractiveness of the market increases;

Masters in Australia attempted this strategy of leveraging on market attractiveness by opening its stores close to Bunnings; it quickly lost the ground (business is now closed) because Bunnings is positioned is like a consulting shop that sells products. (The staff are very well trained to help the buyers.) Masters was focusing on selling products relevant to buyers; however, staff was not as trained at the same level as Bunnings.

If caught in such a competitive scenario answers to thwart competitive threat can be very simple however requires a radical approach of taking a step back and finding the purpose[42].

If you run a café, consider having free Wi-Fi, newspapers, news channels, or heating/cooling, all of which encourage

---

[42] From Purpose to Impact, Nick Craig, Scott A. Snook, HBR, May 2014

patrons to sit down in a comfortable environment and increase their discretionary spend.

Price competition seldom helps, while helping one of our clients who ran a food chain, we noted that though they were price-competing with the market, their cost base was higher; instead of takeaway, they were encouraging their patrons to dine in for lunch. This reduced the number of available seats for high-propensity patrons shrinking the profitability of the business.

While travelling in Mumbai India, I have seen a common practice whereby the same food is served at different price points in two parts of the restaurant offering a different level of service. This is a highly successful model. Though food at the low-cost and high-cost end of the restaurant comes from the same kitchen and is cooked in the same pot, you are paying for the service and you get what you pay for.

CHAPTER 10

Final Thoughts

The purpose of this book is to instigate a line of questioning that challenges you to think about your business from a different lens. Whether you find it confronting, intimidating or exciting, its purpose is to pave the way to your business success:

I will be successful in my endeavour if

- You have started questioning.
- You have started validating.
- You have started measuring.
- You have started benchmarking.

Your business can improve its chances of success if it makes informed decisions about the strategic steps it takes.

This is the end of the book, but not the end of our work together for any question send me an email at sbabbar@sameerbabbar.com.

It has been my honour to serve you and I hope it helps you dare mighty dreams.

This book was written with a mainly bricks-and-mortar store in consideration (though it does touch on aspects of online business). By taking an aspect, or entirety of the business online you can change the game yet again. If you are interested in the topic, or discussion drop me a note.

Disclaimer: Read the book at your own risk, or risk not reading it.   The choice is yours.

Index

D

T

www.ingramcontent.com/pod-product-compliance
Lightning Source LLC
Chambersburg PA
CBHW060303220326
41598CB00027B/4222